A Discography of TREBLE VOICE RECORDINGS

Compiled by
JAMES LASTER

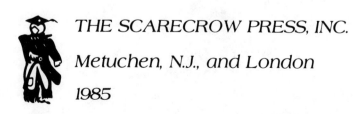

THE SCARECROW PRESS, INC.

Metuchen, N.J., and London

1985

Library of Congress Cataloging in Publication Data

Laster, James, 1934–
    A discography of treble voice recordings.

    Bibliography: p.
    1. Vocal music--Discography. I. Title.
ML156.4.V7L4 1985   016.7899'124   84-22179
ISBN 0-8108-1760-8

TABLE OF CONTENTS

PREFACE

A Discography Of Treble Voice Recordings began as a small
card file as part of an attempt to locate recordings of choral
works performed by women's vocal ensembles for either the Howe
Library of Shenandoah College and Conservatory of Music, or for
the writer's own collection. Early in the collecting process it
was evident that one should not be limited to recordings
performed by women's voices, but should expand the scope to
include recordings by treble voices. In that way, one could
include recordings of ensembles by boys' voices, girls' voices
or children's choirs made up of boys and girls, as well as the
original idea of recordings for women's voices.

"Treble" usually refers to the upper vocal parts of a
choral score. It can also take on the English connotation and
refer to boys' voices and the part they sing in the all-male
choirs of English Cathedrals. The label, boys' choirs, causes
a terminology problem, as one usually thinks of a boys' choir
as being an ensemble where just the soprano and/or alto parts
are sung by unchanged male voices. There are recordings of
boys' choirs which incorporate the changed male voice, thus
giving tenor and baritone parts to the sound. In this
Discography the word "treble" refers either to choirs of unchanged male voices, to choirs of girls' voices, or to choirs
of women's voices.

The search for appropriate recordings began with the
examination of Schwann Record Catalogues, and the Union
Catalogue of the Library of Congress. Record reviews were found
in various periodicals, including, Notes of the American Library
Association, and Fanfares, when available. The series of
recordings of English Cathedral Choirs on Abbey and Alpha labels
often have a cut where the boys (trebles) perform alone.
Examples of mixed-voice ensembles which have a selection
performed by the women of the choir, are included when known.

Another area of recordings examined were those private or
custom recordings made by colleges and high schools. In the
summer of 1982, questionnaires were sent to all directors of
women's choral ensembles whose names appeared on the list
compiled by Sister Sharon Breden, past Chairperson of the
National Committee on Women's Choruses of the American Choral
Directors Association. These directors were asked if their

v

ensembles had made recordings; and if so, what were the
selections contained on the recording. They were also asked if
the recording were still available and how it might be obtained.
Many directors replied to the questionnaire, and the information
has been entered into the <u>Discography</u>. Some directors indicated
that while they had tapes of their ensemble's concerts or
performances, they had not been made into discs or cassettes
which were available as private pressings. This information was
not included. Others replied that although they had made no
recordings, they would be interested in obtaining a copy of the
listing when it was completed.

In addition to the mailing of the questionnaires, the
author visited the sound collections of: The Library of
Congress; the Sibley Library of the Eastman School of Music;
the Library of the School of Music of the University of North
Carolina, Chapel Hill; the Library of the University of North
Carolina-Greensboro, Greensboro, North Carolina; the Library
of the College/Conservatory of Music, University of Cincinnati;
the Talbot Library of Westminster Choir College; and the record
library of radio station WGMS of Washington, D.C.

All the material in the <u>Discography</u> is listed alphabetically
by composer. For each entry, the following format has been
adopted:

    (1)   BRAHMS, Johannes (1833-1897)
          (2)   Ave Maria, Op. 12
          (3)   North German Radio Chorus
          (4)   Gunter Jena, cond.
          (5)   Brahms Choral Works -- Deutsche Grammophon
                2741.018 (date)

    (1)   Composer and/or arranger; and dates if available.
          (2)   Title of work. (For compositions containing
                several movements, separate titles are given.)
          (3)   Name of performing ensemble.
          (4)   Name of conductor.
          (5)   Name of recording (if given) -- Recording
                company and number. If date of issue is
                available, this is given in parenthesis.

                An (*) at the beginning of line five of the
                citation indicates a private-pressing.
                Addresses of the directors and/or ensembles
                are found at the end of the <u>Discography</u>.

The writer would like to express his appreciation to
Shenandoah College and Conservatory of Music for the Faculty
Enrichment Grant which helped intiate this work, and to all who
so willingly assisted; such as the people of WETA-FM, Washington,
D.C., who so graciously gave record information over the phone

when an example was played on the air which fit the criteria of
the Discography; to Clifford Hill for the list of recordings
from his private collection; and to Michael Moody for the
listing of recordings containing cuts sung by the Women of the
Mormon Tabernacle Choir. A very special word of appreciation is
expressed to my son, Travis, for his patience in struggling to
teach me how to use the computer on which the data for this
document was stored; and finally to Marjorie Edmondson, who
typed the final manuscript.

The information contained in the Discography is by no means
complete or comprehensive. It does represent the work of many
choral ensembles and the results of their efforts in recording
the literature written for treble-voice ensembles. Perhaps it
will encourage more groups to record other examples of this
music.

JHL

A

DISCOGRAPHY

OF

TREBLE VOICE RECORDINGS

ADVENT CAROL
    People Look East (Besancon melody)
        Philomela
        Susan Ames-Zierman, dir.
        Make We Joy -- PR 001

AGAY, Denes (1911-   )
    Old Irish Blessing
        Lyons Township High School Treble Choir
        Lynne Bradley, dir.
        *Friends -- Delta DRS-81M 102 (1981)

    Irish Blessing
        Lyons Township High School Treble Choir
        Lynne Bradley, dir.
        *Bursting Out -- Delta DRS-82M-116 (1982)

AHNFELT, Oscar
    Day By Day
        Bethel College Women's Choir
        Oliver Mogck, dir.
        *Gold Cover -- ARK-4250-3

AICHINGER, Gregor (1565-1628)
    Laudate Dominum
        Hungarian Radio Children's Choir
        Botka & Csanyi, conds.
        Hungaroton SLPX 12163

    Regina Coeli
        East Carolina University Women's Glee Club
        Rhonda Fleming, dir.
        *HIS Recording

ALSATIAN FOLK SONG
    Schwerfelholzle (Matches)
        Obernkirchen Children's Choir
        Edith Moeller, cond.
        Songs and A Wonderful Story -- Angel 35684

ALVAD, Thomas
     Maria Gennem Torne Ger
          Lyons Township High School Treble Chorus
          Lynne Bradley, dir.
          *Friends -- Delta DRS 81M-105 (1981)

AMERICAN CAROL
     Shepherds, Rejoice (from White And King's Sacred Harp)
          Philomela
          Susan Ames-Zierman, dir.
          Make We Joy -- PR 001

AMERICAN FOLK SONG
     Wondrous Love (arr. Paul Christiansen)
          Bethel College Women's Choir
          Oliver Mogck, dir.
          *(1972)

AMERICAN HYMN
     Joy To The World (tune PAXTON)
          Philomela
          Susan Ames-Zierman, dir.
          Make We Joy -- PR 001

ANDERSEN, Arthur (arr.) (1880-1958)
     In Heaven Above
          Bethel College Women's Chorus
          Mary Fall, cond.
          *(1979) TAT 9159

ANDRIESSEN, Hendrick (1892-1981)
     Kyrie-Sanctus (Missa Simplex)
          Wells College Choir
          Crawford R. Thoburn, dir.
          *(1979-80)

ANONYMOUS
     Alma Redemptoris Mater (Plainsong)
          London Oratory Junior Choir
          John Holmes, dir.
          Abbey MVP-782

ANONYMOUS (13th c.)
     Ave Maris Stella (Hymn)
          The Boston Camerata
          John Cohen, dir.
          A Medieval Christmas -- Nonesuch H 71315

ANONYMOUS (arr. Comfort Hinderlie-Dalle)
     Away In A Manger
          Women of Mormon Tabernacle Choir
          Cornwall, dir.
          Mormon Tabernacle Choir Sings Christmas Carols --
               Columbia ML 5222

ANONYMOUS (15th c.)
    Cracovia Civitas
        Boys Choir of the Pomeranian Philharmonia
        Stanislaw Galonski, cond.
        Polish Medieval Music -- MHS OR 341

ANONYMOUS (13th c.)
    Gedeonis area (Conductus)
        The Boston Camerata
        John Cohen, dir.
        A Medieval Christmas -- Nonesuch H 71315

ANONYMOUS
    In The Hay By The Oxen's Trough
        The Tapiola Choir
        Erkki Pohjola, dir.
        Tapiolan Joulu 2 -- BIS LP-132

ANONYMOUS (c. 1350)
    Io son un pellegrin
        Vassar Madrigal Singers
        E. Harold Greer, cond.
        The Italian Madrigals: Ars Nova and the 16th c. --
            Allegro Records ALG 3029

ANONYMOUS
    I Was Glad
        Choir of the School of St. Mary & St. Anne
        Llywella Harris, dir.
        Day By Day -- Argo ZRG 785

ANONYMOUS (14th c.)
    Lullay, Lullow: I Saw A Sweete Seemly Sight
        Boys of All Saints, Margaret St.
        Michael Fleming, choirmaster
        Of Glad Tidings -- Book Of The Month Record 11-6521

ANONYMOUS
    Maria, The Lord's Little Maid
        The Tapiola Choir
        Erkki Pohjola, dir.
        Tapiolan Joulu 2 -- BIS LP-132

ANONYMOUS
    Oh Nightingale, come!
        The Tapiola Choir
        Erkki Pohjola, dir.
        Tapiolan Joulu 2 -- BIS LP-132

ANONYMOUS (15th c.)
    O Najdrozszy Kwiatku (O Dearest Flower)
        Women of Pomeranian Philharmonia of Bydgoszcz
        Stanislaw Galonski, cond.
        MHS OR-341

ANONYMOUS
      Rejoice In The Lord Alway
            Chapel Choir of the Blue School, Birmingham
            Hugh Shelton, dir.
            Abbey LPB 766

ANONYMOUS (14th c.)
      Resonemus Laudibus
            Boys Of All Saints, Margaret St.
            Michael Fleming, choirmaster
            Now Make We Merthe -- Decca ZRG-526; Of Glad Tidings --
                  Book Of The Month Record 11-6521

ANONYMOUS
      The Wind Is In The North
            Choir of the School of St. Mary & St. Anne
            Llywela Harris, dir.
            Day By Day -- Argo ZRG 785

ANONYMOUS
      Virsi 14 (I Kneel Down At Your Manger)
            The Tapiola Choir
            Erkki Pohjola, cond.
            Tapiolan Joulu 2 -- BIS LP-132

APPALACHIAN CAROL
      Guide Me O Thou Great Jehovah
            Boys of National Cathedral
            Richard Dirksen, dir.
            *Laudate Dominum -- Cathedral Archives Recording
                  CAR 007

APPALACHIAN FOLK SONG (arr. Leslie Ball)
      Red Rosey Bush
            The Shawnee Choir
            Earl Willhoite, dir.
            Shawnee Showcase Vol II

ARCADELT, Jacques (1505-1568)
      Ave Maria
            Lyons Township High School Treble Choir
            Lynne Bradley, dir.
            *(1975) -- Delta DRS-75-423

ARCH, Gwen (arranger)
      All My Trials
            Cheltenham Ladies' College Choir
            Dorothy Dickinson, dir.
            Cantique -- Alpha APS 321

      Donna, Donna
            Cheltenham Ladies' College Choir
            Dorothy Dickinson, dir.
            Cantique -- Alpha APS 321

Jamaica Farewell
        Cheltenham Ladies' College Choir
        Dorothy Dickinson, dir.
        Cantique -- Alpha APS 321

ARGENTO, Dominick (1927-   )
    Tria Carmina Paschalia
        Dale Warland Singers
        250 Years Of Great Choral Music -- MHS-4358; also
            Augsburg 23-1454

ASCHEN/MARTIN
    Rainbow Connection
        Lyons Township High School Treble Choir
        Lynne Bradley, dir.
        *Bursting Out -- Delta DRS-82M-116 (1982)

AXTOR, Hoyt (arr. Michael Braz)
    Joy To The World
        Miami Boy Choir
        Paul A. Eisenhart, dir.
        *Crest -- ACD-81-3B; Crest S-ACDA-804B

BABBITT, Milton (b. 1916)
    Four Canons from Birthday Canons for Carl Engel
        The University of California - Santa Barbara Dorians
        Michael Ingham, cond.
        *A Program of Music for Women's Voices from the 20th
            Century -- Aea 1094

BACH, J.S. (1685-1750)
    Blessing, Glory and Wisdom
        School Sisters of St. Francis
        S. Marie Gnader, dir.
        *Rhapsody of Praise (St. Joseph Convent)

    Come Gracious Spirit
        Philomela
        Susan Ames-Zierman, dir.
        Make We Joy -- PR 001

    (Den Tod, Den Tod from Christ lag in Todesbanden)
    O'er Death No Man Prevail (chorus #2 of Cantata #4)
        London Oratory Junior Choir
        John Hoban, dir.
        Abbey MVP 782

        (Also SEE recordings of Cantata #4 as a Complete Work)
        EX: Westphalian Singers
             N. Harmoncourt, dir.
             Vanguard S225

Denn das Gesetz des Geistes (Trio from Motet III, Jesu,
        meine Freude, BWV 227)
    (SEE: recordings of Bach Motet III as a complete work.)
    EX: Westminster Choir
         W. Ehmann, cond.
         Peters PLE 1245

Domine Deus (Mass in G)
    The Tapiola Choir
    Erkki Pohjola, dir.
    DG 2530.812

Gloria in Excelsis Deo
    The Choral Ensemble Of Salem College
    Paul Peterson, dir.
    *The Choral Ensemble Of Salem College in Concert --
        XTV 62399

Jehovah, I Would Sing Thy Praise
    Mississippi University for Women Chapel Choir
    Marilyn Swingle, dir.
    *

Jesu, Joy of Man's Desiring (Cantata 147) (arr. Myra Hess)
    Peninsula Women's Chorus
    Patricia Hennings, dir.
    *Song of Survival

Jesu, Joy of Man's Desiring (Cantata 147) (arr. Treharne)
    Moody Women's Glee Club
    Robert Carbaugh, dir.
    *Moody IV -- Moody Bible Institute

Let Me Praise Jesus (Naain Jessusta vain)
    The Tapiola Choir
    Erkki Johjola, dir.
    Tapiolan Joulu 2 -- BIS LP-132

My Spirit Be Joyful
    Women Of The Mormon Tabernacle Choir
    Richard Condie, cond.
    The Mormon Tabernacle Choir At The Worlds Fair --
        Columbia Ms 6619

    The University Choir
    Richard Cox, dir.
    *Christmas Concert 1964 -- CSS 424-1598 B

O Jesu So Sweet
    Wheaton College Women's Chorale
    Mary Hopper, cond.
    *Let All The World In Every Corner Sing -- WETN 820-501

Puer Natus In Bethlehem
        The Tapiola Choir
        Erkki Pohjola, cond.
        Tapiolan Joulu 2 -- BIS LP 132

Rejoice In God, O Ye Righteous
        Mississippi University for Women Chapel Choir
        Marilyn Swingle, dir.
        *

Suscepit Israel (Magnificat BWV 243)
        (SEE recordings of Magnificat as a complete work.)
        EX: Munich Bach Choir
              Karl Richter, cond.
              Munich Bach Choir -- SAPM 198197

Wir Eilen Mit Schwachen, doch emsigen schritten (Cantata 79)
        The Aeolian Singers
        Claire Wall, dir.
        *The Impossible Dream Come True

        Salem College Choral Ensemble
        Paul W. Peterson, cond.
        *On The Campus and On The Road -- CM LP 1006

        Wheaton College Women's Chorale
        Mary Hopper, dir.
        *Let All The World In Every Corner Sing -- WETN 820 50

BACKER/DAVIS/COOK/GREENAWAY (arr. Barry Rose)
    I'd Like To Teach The World To Sing
        St. Paul's Cathedral Boys Choir
        Rejoice -- K-Tel (1980) NE 1067

BACON, Ernst (1898-   )
    Precepts of Angelus Silesius
        The University of California - Santa Barbara Dorians
        Michael Ingham, cond.
        *A Program of Music for Women's Voices from the 20th
            Century -- AEA 1094

BAIN, James (arr. Gordon Jacob)
    Brother James' Air
        Chapel Choir of the Blue-Coat School, Birmingham
        Hugh Shelton, dir.
        Abbey LPB 645

        Mississippi University for Women Chapel Choir
        Marilyn Swingle, dir.
        *

        St. Paul's Cathedral Boys Choir
        Rejoice -- K-Tel (1980) NE-1065

BAKSA, Robert
    Songs of Late Summer (1. Falling Leaves; 2. Willows;
        3. Dawn)
        Miami Girls Chorus
        Lynne Huff, cond.
        *HIS Recording

    Three Spanish Ballads (1. Come At Dawn; 2. Moon Song;
        3. May)
        Miami Girls Chorus
        Lynne Huff, cond.
        *HIS Recording

BANCHIERI, Antonio (1568-1634)
    Io son bella e favorita (from Saviezza giovanile)
        Vassar Madrigal Singers
        E. Harold Geer, cond.
        The Italian Madrigals: Ars Nova and the 16th c. --
            Allegro Records alg 3029

    Scenes from La Pazzia Senile (1. Strazz' e ciabatte;
            2. Misera che farai di Doralice?; 3. Pantalon,
            che vosta far?; 4. Tre villanelle)
        Vassar Madrigal Singers
        E. Harold Geer, cond.
        The Italian Madrigals: Ars Nova and the 16th c. --
            Allegro Records alg 3029

BARAB, Seymour (1921-   )
    First Person Feminine (The Kiss, The Look, Pierrot)
        Choir Of Mary Baldwin College
        Gordon Page, dir.
        *Richmond Sound Stage 10725

BARDOS, Lajos (1899-   )
    Blow The Pipe
        Female and Children's Chorus of Hungarian Radio & TV
        Hungaroton SLPX 11538

    Dana, Dana
        The Tapiola Choir
        Erkki Pohjola, cond.
        Deutsche Gramaphone -- DG 2530.812

    From The Children's Chorus
        Female and Children's Chorus of Hungarian Radio & TV
        Hungaroton SLPX 11538

    In Memory Of Bartok (1965)
        Budapest Kodaly Zoltan Female Chorus
        Ilona Andor, cond.
        Contemporary Hungarian Female Choirs -- Hungaraton
            SLPX 11764

Tavunga
    Female and Children's Chorus of Hungarian Radio & TV
    Hungaroton SLPX 11538

Tunde Song
    Female and Children's Chorus of Hungarian Radio & TV
    Hungaroton SLPX 11538

BART, Lionel (b. 1930) (arr. Leyden)
    Who Will Buy (Oliver)
        Lyons Township High School Treble Choir
        Lynne Bradley, Dir.
        *(1975) -- Delta DRS 75-423

BARTOK, Bela (1881-1945)
    Bird Song (Madardal)
        Kodaly Girls Choir
        Ilona Andor, cond.
        Angel S 36334

    Breadbaking (Ciposutes)
        The Budapest Children's Choir
        Laszlo Czanyi, cond.
        The Budapest Children's Choir at Carnegie Hall (1966)
            -- Victor LM 2861

        Kodaly Girls Choir
        Ilona Andor, cond.
        Angel S 36334

    Don't Leave Me
        Wheaton College Women's Chorale
        Mary Hopper, cond.
        Let All The World In Every Corner Sing -- WETN 820-50

    Enchanting Song
        Budapest Children's Choir
        Laszlo Czanyi, cond.
        Budapest Children's Choir at Carnegie Hall (1966) --
            Victor LM 2861

        The University Of North Carolina Choir
        Richard Cox, dir.
        *Twentieth Century Compositions For Treble Voices --
            CSS 554

        Westover Glee Club
        Robert Harvey, cond.
        *

Five Hungarian Folk Songs
      (Cattle Song; Regret; Courting; Grief; Mocking
      a Boy)
    Radcliffe Choral Society
    Beverly Taylor, cond.
    AKFA Records SK 4672

Regret (Banar)
    Kodaly Girls Choir
    Ilona Andor, cond.
    Angel S 36334

Six Chants Populaires Hongrois
    Maitrise d'enfants
    Jacques Jonineau, cond.
    Pathe DTX 247

Sorrow
    The Budapest Children's Choir
    Laszlo Czanyi, cond.
    The Budapest Children's Choir at Carnegie Hall (1966)
       -- Victor LM 2861

Spring
    Wheaton College Women's Chorale
    Mary Hopper, cond.
    *Let All The World In Every Corner Sing -- WETN 820-50

Spur Dance (Kannustanssi)
    The Tapiola Choir
    Erkki Pohjola, dir.
    Sounds Of Tapiola -- Columbia 5E-062-34670

Tanzlied
    Ensemble Luenica
    Stegan Klimo, cond.
    Chore - RCA PRL 1-9059 (1976)

Teasing Song
    Budapest Children's Choir
    Laszlo Czanyi, cond.
    The Budapest Children's Choir at Carnegie Hall (1966)
       -- Victor LM 2861

    Obernkirchen Children's Choir
    Edith Moeller, cond.
    Songs and a Wonderful Story -- Angel 35684

Three Village Scenes (Wedding; Lullaby; Lad's Dance)
       Budapest Radio Choir
       Gyorgy Lehel, cond.
       Westminster WST 170024

       Budapest Radio Choir
       Gyorgy Lehel, cond.
       Music Guild MS 198 (1970); Westminster Gold WGS-8210

       Gyor Girl's Chorus
       Anatal Dorati, cond.
       Hungaroton SLPX 11510

Vocal Music -4- 27 2-&-3 Part Choruses (1935) Contents:
           Spring; Don't Leave Here; Enchanting Song;
           Letters To Those At Home; Play Song; Courting;
           Hey, You Hawk; Don't Leave Me; I Have A Ring; I've
           No One In The World; Breadbaking; Hussar Loafer's
           Song; Wandering; Girl's Teasing Song; Boy's
           Teasing Song; Michaelmas Congratulations; Suitor;
           Grief; Bird Song; Jeering; Regret; Had I Not Seen
           You; The Bird Flew Away; Pillow Dance; Canon;
           God Be With You
       Female Choir Of The Music High School, Gyor
       Miklos Szabo, dir.
       Hungaroton LPX 1290

Vocal Music - 27 Choruses (selection: Don't Leave Me;
           Hussar; Bread Baking; Loafer; Enchanting Song;
           Teasing Song; Only Tell Me; The Wooing Of A Girl)
       The Concert Choir
       Margaret Hillis, dir.
       Bartok Records 312 (1955)

Wandering (Bolyongas)
       Kodaly Girls Choir
       Ilona Andor, cond.
       Angel S 36334

The Wooing Of A Girl
       Lyons Township High School Treble Choir
       Lynne Bradley, dir.
       *(1977) -- Delta DRS 77m 621

BEETHOVEN, L. (1770-1827)
    Gott ist mein Lied
       Vienna Choir Boys
       Romantic Vienna -- Everest SDBR 3240

    Hallelujah from Mount Of Olives (Arr. Geer)
       The University Choir
       Richard Cox, dir.
       *Christmas Concert 1963 -- CSS 276 1530 A

King Stephen Op. 117 (Chorus #4)
    Chorus of the Hungarian Radio & TV
    Genza Oberfrank, cond.
    Hungaroton LPX 1474

Minuet in G
    Peninsula Women's Chorus
    Patricia Hennings, dir.
    *Songs of Survival

BELLASIO, Paolo (1554-1594)
    Quel Tristaret d'Amore
        Westover Glee Club
        Robert Harvey, cond.
        *

BENNET, John (1575?-1614)
    All Creatures Now
        Choir and School of S. Mary and S. Anne
        Llywela Harris, cond.
        In Quires and Places #5 -- Abbey LPB 668

BENNETT, Richard Rodney (1936-   )
    Dormi Jesu
        The Elizabethan Singers
        Louis Halsey, cond.
        Of Glad Tidings -- Book Of The Month Records 11-6521

    Lullabies
        Choristers Of Worcester Cathedral
        Abbey LPB 764 (1976)

BERKLEY, Lennox (1903-   )
    Salve Regina
        The London Oratory Junior Choir
        John Hobar, dir.
        Laetare Jerusalem -- Abbey MVP 782

BERLIN, Irving (1888-   )
    Alexander's Rag-Time Band
    Happy Holidays
        The Salem Academy Glee Club
        Jean Burroughs, dir.
        *(1978-1979) -- Recorded Publications Z-5300-71

BERLOIZ, Hector (1803-1869)
    Priere du Matin
    Tantum Ergo
        Heinrich Scheutz Choir & Chorale
        Roger Norrington, dir.
        Songs For Chorus -- ARGO ZRG 635

BERNHARD, Christoph (1627-1692)
Was betrubst du dich, meine Seele
The Collegium Sagittarii
Derek McUlloch, dir.
Oryx -- EXO 26

BERNSTEIN, Leonard (1918-   )
One Hand, One Heart (West Side Story)
Salem College Choral Ensemble
Paul W. Peterson, dir.
*On The Campus and On The Road -- CM LP 1006

West Side Story selections (I Feel Pretty; Somewhere; One
Hand, One Heart; Tonight)
The Choral Ensemble of Salem College
Paul Peterson, dir.
*The Choral Ensembles Of Salem College In Concert --
XTV 62399

BILLINGS, William (1746-1800)
Shepherds Carol (arr. Thoburn)
The Wells College Choir
Crawford Thoburn, dir.
*(1980-1981)

BINKHERD, Gordon (1916-   )
On The King's Highway (Pater Noster; Little Things;
Hespereus; The White Swan)
Glen Ellyn Children's Chorus
Doreen Rao, dir.
*Crest Records -- NC-ACDA-80-8B

BLISS, Sir Arthur (1891-1975)
A Prayer To The Infant Jesus (1968)
Ambrosian Singers
Philip Ledger, cond.
PRS-80th Birthday Celebration -- MHS 3096

Choir & School Of S. Mary And S. Anne
Llywela Harris, dir.
In Quires and Places #5 -- Abbey LPB 668

BOHM, G.
Calm As The Night (arr. Cain)
Women of Mormon Tabernacle Choir
Richard Condie, cond.
Old Beloved Songs -- Columbia MS-7012

BOULANGER, Lili (1893-1918)
Pie Jesu
Chorale Elizabeth Brasseau
Everest LP BR 6059 (SD=SDBR 3059)

BOYCE, William (1710-1779)
 Alleluia
   Hungarian Radio Children's Choir
   Botka & Csanyi, conds.
   Hungaroton SLPX 12163

 The Sorrow Of My Heart
   Norwich Cathedral Choir
   Nicholas
   In Quires and Places, #9 -- Abbey LPB 718

BRAHMS, Johannes (1833-1897)
 Ave Maria, Op. 12
   Budapest Kodaly Female Choir
   Ilona Andor, cond.
   Hungaroton SLPX 11691 (1976)

   East Carolina University Women's Glee Club
   Rhonda Fleming, dir.
   *HIS Recording

   North German Radio Choir
   Gunter Jena, cond.
   Brahms Choral Works -- Deutsche Grammophon 2741-018

   Schutz Choir of London
   Roger Norrington, dir.
   Geistliche Chormusik -- Carus Verlag FSM 53128,
    FSM 53129

   The University Choir
   Richard Cox, cond.
   *Christmas Concert 1967 -- Robbins Recording 1911-A

   Weiner Sangerknaben
   Phillips PHS 9000002

 Barcarole (#3 of Twelve Songs & Romances, Op. 44)
   Student Madrigal Choir, Munster
   Herma Kramm, cond.
   Musical Heritage Society -- MHS 3668 (1977)

 Bird In Air Will Stray Afar
   Alabama Music Educators Association All State
   Hugh Thomas, dir.
   *All State Grand Concert 1978 -- USC Sound Enterprise

 Blessed Are They That Dwell In Thy House
   New Mexico All State Girl's Chorus
   John D. Raymond, dir.
   *New Mexico All State 1968 -- Century Stereo 29256

der Brautigam (#2 of Twelve Songs & Romances)
    Student Madrigal Choir, Munster
    Herma Kramm, cond.
    Musical Heritage Society MHS 3668 (1977)

Four Songs, Op. 17
    Budapest Kodaly Female Choir
    Ilona Andor, cond.
    Hungaroton SLPX 11691 (1976)

    Chorus of Orchestra de Paris
    Arthur Oldhis, cond.
    M & C Records 7008 (digital)

    Gachinger Kantorei
    H. Rilling, cond.
    CMR-Oryx-3C-324

    Hanover Women's Choir
    Ludwig Rutt, cond.
    Camerata -- CMS 30.068 LPT

    Musica Aeterna Chamber Chorus
    Frederic Waldman, cond.
    Musica Aeterna At Alice Tully Hall -- Decca DL-79437
        (1971)

    North German Radio Chorus
    Gunter Jena, cond.
    Brahms Choral Works -- Deutsche Grammophon 2741-018

    Vienna Academy Choir
    Rheinhold Schmid, cond.
    Westminster W-9617; also Westminster WL-50 (1950)

From Yon Hills In Torrents Speeds
    Alabama Music Educators Association All State
    Hugh Thomas, dir.
    *All State Grand Concert 1978 -- USC Sound Enterprise

How Lovely Is Thy Dwelling (Requiem)
    The Sullins Choir
    Leon B. Fleming, Jr., dir.
    Recorded Publications E4QL2071 (1953-1954)

The Hunter
    Lyons Township High School Treble Choir
    Lynne Bradley, dir.
    *Friends -- Delta DRS 81M 105 (1981)

Make In Me A Clean Heart (from Op. 29, #2)
    Mississippi University for Women Chapel Choir
    Marilyn Swingle, dir.
    *

Marienlieder, Op. 22
    Vienna Kammerchor
    Reinhold Schmid, cond.
    Westminster WL-50 (1950)

Nightingale, The Sweetest Song
    Alabama Music Educators Association All State
    Hugh Thomas, dir.
    *All State Grand Concert -- USC Sound Enterprise

Psalm 13, Op. 27
    Bethel College Women's Choir
    Oliver Mogek, dir.
    *(1972) -- ARK 2131-3

    Budapest Kodaly Female Choir
    Ilona Andor, cond.
    Hungaroton SLPX 11691 (1976)

    North German Radio Chorus
    Gunter Jena, cond.
    Brahms Choral Works -- Deutsche Grammophon 2741-018

    Schutz Choir of London
    Roger Norrington, dir.
    Geistliche Chormusik -- Carus Verlag FSM 53128,
        FSM 53129

    University Choir
    Richard Cox, dir.
    *Christmas Concert, 1965 -- Copeland Sound Studios CSS
        572-2103-A

    Wiener Sangerknaben
    Furthmoser, cond.
    Doblinger

Songs for Treble Voices (arr. H. Ades)
        (contains: 1. Questions (Fragen); The Bride (Die
        Braut); The Bridegroom (Der Brautigam)
    Miami Girls Chorus
    Lynne Huff, cond.
    *HIS Recording

Thirteen Canons, Op. 113
    North German Radio Chorus
    Gunter Jena, cond.
    Brahms Choral Works -- Deutsche Grammophon 2741-018

Three Motets, Op. 37
      (only #1 O Gracious Jesus; #2 We Adore Thee)
      Bethel College Women's Choir
      Mary Fall, cond.
      *(1979) -- TAT 9159

      Budapest Kodaly Female Choir
      Ilona Andor, cond.
      Hungaroton SLPX 11691 (1976)

      North German Radio Chorus
      Gunter Jena, cond.
      Brahms Choral Works -- Deutsche Grammophon 2741-018

      Schutz Choir of London
      Roger Norrington, dir.
      Geistliche Chormusik -- Carus Verlag FSM 53128,
          FSM 53129

      Wells College Choir
      Crawford R. Thoburn, dir.
      *(1979-80)

Three Motets, Op. 110
      Schutz Choir of London
      Roger Norrington, dir.
      Geistliche Chormusik -- Carus Verlag FSM 53128,
          FSM 53129

Twelve Songs and Romances, Op. 44
      Budapest Kodaly Female Choir
      Ilona Andor, cond.
      Hungaroton SLPX 11691

      (#7-#10 only)
      Monteverdi Choir
      Einfeldt, cond.
      Telefunken SLT-43100

      North German Radio Chorus
      Gunter Jena, cond.
      Brahms Choral Works -- Deutsche Grammophon 2741-018

      (#7-#10)
      Vienna Choir Boys
      Hans Gillesberger, dir.
      Vienna Choir Boys Serenade -- RCA-PRL-1-9034

We Love The Place, O God
      Choir of the School of St. Mary & St. Anne
      Llywela Harris, dir.
      Day By Day -- Argo ZRG 785

Within My Heart Breathes Music (arr. Gibb)
 Shenandoah Chorus
 Robert McSpadden, cond.
 *Festival of Music 1966 -- Custom Stereo V255753

Zu Strassburg auf der Schanz
 Student Madrigal Choir, Munster
 Herma Kramm, cond.
 Folksongs For Women's Voices -- Musical Heritage Society
  MHS3668

BRAZILIAN CHRISTMAS SONGS
 Natal brasileiro
  Cancrinhos de Petropolis
  Aleco Bocchino, dir.
  Radio Ministerio da Educacao e Cultura -- PRA-Z1003

BRIGHT, Houston (1916-1970)
 Four Sacred Songs For The Night
  (1. Evening; 2. Nightfall; 4. Sunrise)
  Lyons Township High School Treble Choir
  Lynne Bradley, dir.
  *(1975) -- Delta DRS 75-423

BRISTOL, Lee Harvey, Jr.
 Let Your Bearing In Life
  Choir of Trinity Church, Princeton
  James Litton, dir.
  Music by 20th Century Composers (American) -- Gamut
   UT-4501

BRITTEN, Benjamin (1913-1976)
 Ceremony Of Carols, Op. 28
  American Boys Choir
  John Kuzma, dir.
  Pro Arte Digital PAD 160

  Highlights From The 1977 Aldeburg Festival
  Columbia M-3-35197

  Choir of S. Mary & S. Anne
  Llywela Harris, dir.
  Ave Maria: A Celebration of Carols -- Alpha ApS 315

  Choristers of Canterbury Cathedral
  Sidney Campbell, dir.
  London 5634

  Copenhagen Boys' Choir
  Benjamin Britten, cond.
  Decca LW 5070

Ceremony Of Carols, Op. 28 (continued)
    Chorus of Orchestra de Paris
    Arthur Oldhis
    M & C Records 70008 (digital)

    Coventry Cathedral Boys Choir
    David Lepine, cond.
    Gloria In Excelsis -- Chapter One CMS 1007

    Kings College Cambridge
    David Willcocks, dir.
    Benjamin Britten - Seraphim S-60217; also EMI-HQS-1285

    Lyons Township High School Treble Choir
    Lynne Bradley, dir.
    *(1979) -- Delta DRS 79M-614

    Boys of National Cathedral, Washington, D.C.
    Paul Calloway, cond.
    *WCFM Recording LP-11

    Choristers of New College, Oxford
    Alpha - ADV 002

    Prague Radio Children's Choir
    Bohumil Kulinsky, cond.
    Crossroads 22 16 0154 (1967); Supraphon SUAST 50757
        (1972)

    St. John's College, Cambridge
    George Guest, cond.
    Benjamin Britten - Argo ZRG 5440

    Women of Robert Shaw Chorale
    Robert Shaw
    RCA-LSC 2759

    Texas Boys Choir
    George Bragg, cond.
    Decca DLT 10.060 (1962); also Turnabout 34544
        (Cassette 2218)

    University Choir
    Richard Cox, dir.
    *Christmas Concert 1967 -- Robbins Recording 1911-A;
        also *Christmas Concert 1963 -- Copland Sound
        Studios CSS 275 1530 A

    University of Virginia Women's Chorus
    Katherine Mitchell, dir.
    *Candlelight Christmas -- 8393

Ceremony Of Carols, Op. 28 (continued)
    Vienna Boys Choir
    BASF - KBB 21232; also RCA - ARL-1-3437

    Winchester Cathedral Choir
    Martin Neary, cond.
    Pye Virtuoso - TPLS-13065

Ceremony Of Carols
      (Wolcom Yole; There Is No Rose; This Little Babe)
    Alabama Music Educators Association Girls' Chorus
    Hugh Thomas, dir.
    *Alabama All State Grand Concert 1978 -- USC Sound
      Enterprise

Christmas Song Of The Women
    Wilbye Consort
    Peter Pears, cond.
    Decca SXL 6487; Decca DS 26527 (1977)

Coaching Song (from The Little Sweep)
    The Budapest Children's Choir
    Laszlo Czanyi, cond.
    The Budapest Children's Choir at Carnegie Hall (1966)
      -- Victor LM 2861

Corpus Christi Carol
    Boys of National Cathedral, Washington, D.C.
    Richard Dirksen, dir.
    *Joy Of Christmas, Vol. II -- Cathedral Archives
      Recording CAR 007

    Coventry Cathedral Boys Choir
    David Lepine, cond.
    Gloria In Excelsis -- Chapter One CMS 1007

Deo Gracias (A Ceremony of Carols)
    The Aeolian Singers
    Claire Wall, dir.
    *The Impossible Dream Come True

    Lyons Township High School Treble Choir
    Lynne Bradley, dir.
    *Patterns In Music -- Delta DRS-74-139A

    Clovis High School Women's Choir
    Wayne Anderson, dir.
    *Clovis High School

Fancie
    New Mexico All State Girls' Chorus
    John D. Raymond, dir.
    *New Mexico All State -- Century Stereo 29256

Friday Afternoon Songs, Op. 7
    Choir of Downside School, Purvey
    Benjamin Britten, cond.
    Decca LXT 6264; London STS 15173

    (Begone Dull Care; I mun Be Married on Sunday; There
        Was A Man Of Newington; Jazz Man)
    Cincinnati Boys Choir
    William Dickinson, dir.
    *Cincinnati Boys Choir Plays Nashville

    (A New Year Carol)
    Coventry Cathedral Boys Choir
    David Lepine, cond.
    Gloria In Excelsis -- Chapter One CMS 1007

Golden Vanity, Op. 78
    Winchester Cathedral Choir
    Martin Neary, cond.
    Pye Virtuoso -- TPLS-13065

Missa Brevis, Op. 63
    American Boys Choir
    John Kuzima, dir.
    Pro Arte Digital -- PAD 160

    Berkshire Boy Choir
    Brian Runnek, music director
    Alleluia -- RCA LSC 3081

    Coventry Cathedral Boys Choir
    David Lepine, cond.
    Gloria In Excelsis -- Chapter One CMS 1007

    Kings College Cambridge
    David Willcocks, cond.
    Benjamin Britten - Seraphim S-60217; also EMI HQS-1285

    Choristers of New College, Oxford
    Alpha - ADV 002

    St. Johns College, Cambridge
    George Guest, cond.
    Benjamin Britten - Argo ZRG-5440; also Decca D112D3

    Choir of St. Thomas, New York
    Gerre Hancock, dir.
    *A Concert in Memory of Benjamin Britten -- St. Thomas

    Women's Choir of University of North Carolina -
        Greensboro
    Richard Cox, dir.
    *Christmas Concert 1974 -- Nation Engineering 7788

Missa Brevis, Op. 63 (continued)
    University of North Carolina Choir
    Richard Cox, dir.
    *Twentieth Century Compositions For Treble Voices --
        Copland Sound Studios CSS-554

    Wandsworth School Boys Choir
    Russell Burgess, dir.
    English Choral Music -- Pye TPLS-13020

    Winchester Cathedral Choir
    Martin Neary, cond.
    Pye Virtuoso -- TPLS 13065

    Worcester Cathedral Choir
    Donald Hunt, dir.
    Worcester Cathedral Choir In Concert -- Alpha ACA 524

New Year Carol
    Choir of Magdalen College, Oxford
    John Harper, dir.
    Alpha ACA 527

Old Abram Brown (from Friday Afternoon Song, Op. 7)
    Cincinnati Boys Choir
    William Dickinson, dir.
    *Now Gentlemen

    Tapiola Children's Choir
    Erikki Pohjola, cond.
    Deutsche Gramophon 2530.812

O Waly, Waly
    Women's Voices of the Elizabethan Singers
    Louis Halsey, cond.
    Argo   ZRG-5496

Psalm 150, Op. 67
    Downside School Choir, Purley
    Benjamin Britten, cond.
    Decca LXT-6264; London STS-15173

    Glen Ellyn Children's Choir
    Doreen Rao, cond.
    *Crest Records -- NC-ACDA-80-8B

Sweet Was The Song (1931)
    Wilbye Consort
    Peter Pears, cond.
    Decca SXL 6487; Decca OS 26527

This Little Babe (Ceremony Of Carols)
  Bethel College Women's Choir
  Oliver Mogck, dir.
  *(1972)

  Clovis High School Women's Choir
  Wayne Anderson, dir.
  *Clovis High School Concert Choir - 1980

Three Two-Part Songs (The Ride By Nights; The Rainbow; The
      Ship Of Rio)
  American Boys Choir
  John Kuzma, dir.
  Pro Arte Digital -- PAD 160

  Walden Trio
    Wilbye Consort
    Peter Pears, cond.
    Decca SXL 6487; Decca DS 26527 (1977)

BROECKX, Jan P. (1880-1965)
  A Christmas Carol
    Choral Ensemble Of Salem College
    Paul Patterson, dir.
    *The Choral Ensemble of Salem College In Concert --
    XTV-62399

BRYAN, Charles (1911-   )
  Charlottown
    Miami Girls Chorus
    Lynne Huff, cond.
    *HIS Recording

BUCHT, Gunnar (1927-   )
  Hund skenar glad (Dog Runs Happy), 1965 (1. Hund skenar
      glad; 2. Hoppa, skratta, bleka, magra; 3. Linnea
      soker jag; 4. Det enkla starka uppen bara; 5. Sag
      vi har ej mer)
    Sveriges Symfoniorkester & Damkor ur Radio Koren
    Stig Westerberg, cond.
    Caprice CAP 1075

BUCK, P. C.
  The Flowering Manger
    Choir of S. Mary & S. Anne
    Llywela Harris, dir.
    Ave Maria: A Celebration of Carols -- Alpha APS 315

BURGON, Geoffrey (1941-   )
  Magnificat and Nunc Dimittis
    HAVE-20

BURKHARD, Paul (1911-1977)
     Kindermesse
          Schuler vom Thurhof
          Paul Burkhard, cond.
          Jecklin ML-D-1004

BURLEIGH, H. T. (1866-1949)
     My Lord, What A Morning
          The Choral Ensemble Of Salem College
          Paul Patterson, dir.
          *The Choral Ensemble Of Salem College In Concert --
               XTV 62399

     Oh Peter, Go Ring-a Dem Bells (arr. Victor Harris)
          Choir and School of S. Mary and S. Anne
          Llywela Harris, dir.
          In Quires And Places #5 -- Abbey LPB 668

BURROUGHS, Bob (arr.) (1937-   )
     Three Early American Hymn Tunes (Holy Manna; Come Thou
               Fount; When I Can Read My Title Clear)
          Bethel College Women's Choir
          Mary Fall, cond.
          *(1976)

BURT, Alfred S.
     Caroling, Caroling
          Cincinnati Boys Choir
          William Dickinson, dir.
          *C.A.C.B.C.

BUTLER, Eugene (1935-   )
     A Praire Woman Sings
          Lyons Township High School Treble Choir
          Lynne Bradley, dir.
          *(1977) -- Delta DRS-77M-621

     Glorificamus
          Lyons Township High School Treble Choir
          Lynne Bradley, dir.
          *Friends -- Delta DRS 81M-105

     In The Highlands
          Clovis High School Treble Tones
          Wayne Anderson, dir.
          *Contest Selections - 1981

BUXTEHUDE, Dietrich (1637-1707)
    Jubilate Domino, omnis terra
        The Collegium Sagittarii
        Derek McUlloch, dir.
        Oryx EXP 26

    Zion Hort die Wachter singen
        Boys' Choir of St. Mary's Hall, Stonyhurst
        Harry Duckworth, dir.
        Pueri Sanctae Mariae -- Alpha APS 322

BYRAM-WIGFIELD, Rebekah
    Christmas Bell Song
        Cheltenham Ladies' College Choir
        Dorothy Dickinson, dir.
        Cantique -- Alpha APS 321

BYRD, William (1543-1623)
    From Virgin's Womb This Day Did Come
        Choir of St. Paul's Cathedral, Purcell Consort Of
            Voices
        Grayston Burgess, dir.
        Argo ZRG-659

        Choir Of St. Michael's College, Tenbury
        Roger Judd, dir.
        The Choir Of St. Michael's College, Tenbury -- Abbey
            ARR 303

    Lullaby
        Lyons Township High School Treble Choir
        Lynne Bradley, dir.
        *(1977) -- Delta DRS-77M-621

    Sing Ye To Our Lord
        The University Choir
        Richard Cox, dir.
        *Christmas Concert 1963 -- Copeland Studios CSS-275-
            1530A

BYSHENK
    Lamb Of God
        Lyons Township High School Treble Choir
        Lynne Bradley, dir.
        *Friends -- Delta DRS 81M-105

CACCINI, O. (16th c.)
    Aure Volanti
        The Salem Academy Glee Club
        Jean Burroughs, dir.
        *(1980-1981) -- Recorded Publication Z 577041

CALDWELL, Mary Elizabeth (1909-   )
     Let Us Follow Him
          First Baptist Church, Tulsa
          James D. Woodward, dir.
          Broadman Records 452-064

     My Constant Joy (arr.)
          Mississippi University for Women Chapel Choir
          Marilyn Swingle, dir.
          *

CAPLET, Andre (1878-1925)
     Mass
          Girls Choir of the O.R.T.F.
          Jacques Jouineau, cond.
          Musical Heritage MHS 1658

     O Salutaris
          Westover Glee Club
          Robert Harvey, cond.
          *Westover

CARMICHAEL, R. (arr. Mary Fall)
     Season Of The Long Rains (American Gospel Song)
          Bethel College Women's Choir
          Mary Fall, cond.
          *(1979)

CARTER, Elliott (1908-   )
     The Harmony Of Morning
          Women of Gregg Smith Singers
          Gregg Smith, cond.
          Vox SVBX 5354

CASALS, Pablo (1876-1973)
     Canco A La Verge
          Choir of the Montserrat Capella
          Dom Irenea M. Segarra, cond.
          Everest 3196

     Eucaristica
          Choir of the Montserrat Capella
          Dom Irenea M. Segarra, cond.
          Pablo Casals At Montserrat -- Everest 3196

          Lyons Township High School Treble Choir
          Lynne Bradley, dir.
          *Bursting Out -- Delta DRS-82M-116

     I Am Black, but Comely (SEE: Nigra Sum)

Nigra Sum
        Lyons Township High School Treble Choir
        Lynne Bradley, dir.
        *Patterns In Music -- Delta DRS-74-139A

        Leeds Parish Church Choir
        Donald Hunt, cond.
        Abbey LPB-754

        Mississippi University for Women Chapel Choir
        Marilyn Swingle, dir.
        *

        Montserrat Capella Choir
        Dom Irenen M. Segarra, cond.
        Everest 3196

CATHOLIC MISSION MUSIC IN CALIFORNIA
    Alabado
        Coro hispanico de Mallorca
        Pedre Juan Thomas, cond.
        New York Society for the Preservation of the American
            Musical Heritage MIA 96 (1959)

CHANT
    TeDeum
        School Sisters of St. Francis
        S. Marie Gnader, dir.
        *Rhapsody of Praise (St. Joseph Convent)

(for additional Chant listings, SEE Gregorian Chant)

CHAPPELL, Herbert
    The Goliath Jazz
        The Southend Boys' Choir
        Michael Crable, dir.
        Vista VPS 1027

CHARLES, E. (1895-   )
    Clouds (Deis)
        Mormon Tabernacle Choir
        Cornwall, cond.
        Songs Of Faith & Devotion -- Columbia ML 5203

CHARPENTIER, Marc Antoine (1645-1704)
    Magnificat (for Port Royal Convent)
        Sopranos of Blanchard Vocal Ensemble
        Nonesuch - H-71040

CHERUBINI, Luigi (1760-1842)
    Ave Maria
        The Sullins Choir
        Leon B. Fleming, Jr., dir.
        Recorded Publications E4QL2071 (1953-1954)

CHIHARA, Paul S. (1938-   )
     Magnificat (1965)
          New England Conservatory
          Lorna Cooke de Varon, cond.
          Composer's Recording CRI-SD-409 (1979)

CHOPIN, Frederic (1810-1849)
     Prelude No. 15, the "Raindrop"
          Peninsula Women's Chorus
          Patricia Hennings, dir.
          *Song of Survival

CHRISTIANSEN, F. Melius (arr.) (1871-1955)
     Lost In The Night
          Bethel College Women's Choir
          Mary Fall, cond.
          *(1976)

     Wondrous Love (Southern Folk Hymn)
          Bethel College Women's Choir
          Oliver Mogck, dir.
          *(1972)

CLAYTON
     We Shall See His Lovely Face
          The Ladies Treble Trio
          *His Glorious Presence - Mennonite Hour Recordings
               MHLP 13-ST

COLE, Laura
     A Special Kind Of Star
          Miami Girls Chorus
          Laura Huff, cond.
          *HIS Recording

COLLINSON, Francis M. (arr.)
     The Prickety Bush
          Choir and School of S. Mary and S. Anne
          Llywella Harris, dir.
          In Quires and Places #5 - Abbey LPB-668

CONDUCTUS (13th c.)
     Beata Viscera
          Wells College Choir
          Crawford R. Thoburn, dir.
          *(1979-80)

     Gedonis area (13th c.)
          The Boston Camerata
          John Cohen, dir.
          A Medieval Christmas -- Nonesuch H 71315

COLEMAN, Cy (1929-   )
    Hey, Look Me Over (Wildcat)
        Salem College Choral Ensemble
        Paul W. Peterson, dir.
        *On The Campus and On The Road - CM LP-1006

CONSTANTINI, Alessandro (1581-1657)
    Confetemini Domino
        The University Choir
        Richard Cox, dir.
        *Christmas Concert 1963 -- Copeland Sound Studio-CSS
            276-1530A

COOKSON
    Go, Song of Mine!
        New Mexico All State Girl's Choir
        John D. Raymond, dir.
        *New Mexico Music Educators Association -- Century
            Stereo 29256

COOPER, Paul
    "?"
        Cincinnati Boys Choir
        William Dickinson, dir.
        *C.A.C.B.C.

COPLAND, Aaron (1900-   )
    An Immortality
        Vienna State Academy Chorus
        William Strickland, cond.
        A Concert Of American Music In Schoenbrunn -- Vox
            PL 7750

    Ching-A-Ring Chaw
        The Budapest Children's Choir
        Laszlo Czanyi, cond.
        The Budapest Children's Choir at Carnegie Hall (1966)
            Victor LM 2861

    Long Time Ago
        The Aeolian Singers
        Claire Wall, dir.
        *The Impossible Dream Comes True

CORFE, Joseph (1741-1820)
    Thou O God Art Raised In Zion
        The London Oratory Junior Choir
        John Hoban, dir.
        Laetare Jerusalem -- Abbey MVP 782

COUPERIN, Francois (1668-1733)
  Christ Is Arisen
    Wheaton College Women's Chorale
    Mary Hopper, cond.
    *Let All The World In Every Corner Sing -- WETN 820-50-1

  Consacrons nos aus
    Choristers of Worcester Cathedral
    Abbey LPB 764

  O Sing Unto The Lord
    Salem College Choral Ensemble
    Paul W. Peterson, dir.
    *On The Campus And On The Road -- CM-LP 1006

COUSINS, M. Thomas (1914-   )
  A Hymn To Truth
    University Of North Carolina Choir
    Richard Cox, dir.
    *Twentieth Century Compositions For Treble Voices --
      CSS 554

COX, David (1916-   )
  The Child Of Life
    Greensboro College Glee Club
    E.L. Williams, dir.
    *Christmas Concert 1967 -- 1913B

COX, Noel (1917-   )
  Oculi omnium (1967)
    Choir and School of S. Mary and S. Anne
    Llywela Harris, dir.
    In Quires and Places #5 -- Abbey LPB 668

CRAM, James D. (1931-1971)
  Lord Your Constant Love
    Wheaton College Women's Chorale
    Mary Hopper, cond.
    *Let All The World In Every Corner Sing -- WETN 820-50-1

  Praise God With Loud Songs
    Wheaton College Women's Chorale
    Mary Hopper, cond.
    *Let All The World In Every Corner Sing -- WETN 820-50-1

  Three Prayers from the Ark (1973)
    Bethel College Women's Choir
    Mary Fall, cond.
    *(1979)

CROO, R.
  The Coventry Carol (arr. B Treharne)
    Ladies of Mormon Tabernacle Choir
    Richard P. Condie, dir.
    The Greatest Christmas Hits -- CBS-37853

CRUSADER'S HYMN
    Fairest Lord Jesus
        Bethel College Women's Choir
        Mary Fall, cond.
        *(1979)

CURRY
    Music, When Soft Voices Die
        New Mexico All State Girls' Choir
        John D. Raymond, dir.
        *New Mexico Music Educators Association 1968 --
           Century Stereo 29256

CZECH CAROL
    Shepherds Awake (arr. Thoburn)
        Wells College Choir
        Crawford R. Thoburn, dir.
        *(1980-81)

CZONKA, Paul (1905-   )
    Concierto de Navidad
        Salem College Chorus
        Janice Harsanyi, cond.
        *Expressions -- STP-001

DALLAPICCOLA, Luigi (1904-1975)
    Canti di Prigionia (1938-1941) (2nd movement for 4-part
           women)
        Monteverdi Choir Of Hamburg
        Jurgens, cond.
        Telefunken 641011

        Tanglewood Festival Chorus
        Oliver, dir.
        Nonesuch 79060

DA NOLA
    Are All the Ladies Deaf
        Washington High School Choirs
        Karen Bushman-Villilo, dir.
        *Spring Concert 1976

DANISH FOLK SONGS
    Contents: Det er i dag et vejr; Se, hvor blaner sommer-
           himlen; Rondeau; Yndigt dufter Danmark; De lyse
           naetter; Trille borens morgensang; Improvisation
           om bord; Hor, nu tader blaesten; Vinter, a vinter;
           Linden sol; Sig naermertiden; Krodus; Begynd
           da'en med en sang
        Danish Radio Girls Choir
        F. Wagner, dir.
        EGTVED EGT-LP-3

DARKE, Harold (1888-1976)
　　Lord's Prayer
　　　　Choristers of Chester Cathedral
　　　　Roger Fisher, dir.
　　　　Vista   VAS 2001

DARST, Glen (1896-   )
　　O God Of Youth
　　　　Mississippi University for Women Chapel Choir
　　　　Marilyn Swingle, dir.
　　　　*

DAVEY, John
　　O Praise God In His Holiness
　　　　Chapel Choir of the Blue-Coat School, Birmingham
　　　　Hugh Shelton, dir.
　　　　Abbey LPB 645

DAVIDSON, Charles (1929-   )
　　I Never Saw Another Butterfly
　　　　Columbia College Choir
　　　　Gutherie Darr, dir.
　　　　*Crest ACD-81-3A

　　　　Columbus Boychoir School
　　　　Donald Hanson, cond.
　　　　*Columbus Boy Choir School CBP-DB 6174a

　　　　Lyons Township High School Treble Choir
　　　　Lynne Bradley, dir.
　　　　*Delta DRS 82M-116

　　　　Miami Boy Choir
　　　　Paul A. Eisenhart, cond.
　　　　*Crest S-ACDA-80-4B

DAVIES, Peter Maxwell (1934-   )
　　O Magnum Mysterium
　　　　Cirencester Grammar School
　　　　P.M. Davies, cond.
　　　　Argo   ZRG 5327

DAVIS, K. K. (1892-1980)
　　As It Fell Upon The Night
　　　　The University Choir
　　　　Richard Cox, dir.
　　　　*Christmas Concert 1964 -- CSS 424-1598

　　Carol of the Drum
　　　　Cincinnati Boys Choir
　　　　William Dickinson, dir.
　　　　*Cincinnati All-City Boys' Choir

Let All Things Now Living (Ash Grove)
    The Sullins Choir
    Leon B. Fleming, Jr., dir.
    Recorded Publications E4QL2071 (1953-1954)

The Little Drummer Boy
    Vienna Choir Boys
    Hans Gillesberger, dir.
    Christmas Festival -- RCA PRL 1-8020

Thou Who Was God
    Alabama Music Educators All State
    Hugh Thomas, dir.
    *Alabama Music Educators Association

    Wheaton College Women's Chorale
    Mary Hopper, dir.
    *Let All The World In Every Corner Sing -- WETN 820-501

DAWSON, William (1898-   )
    Aina' That Good News
        Lyons Township High School Treble Choir
        Lynne Bradley, dir.
        *Bursting Out -- Delta DRS 82M-116

    Jesus Walked This Lonesome Valley
        The Choral Ensemble Of Salem College
        Paul Peterson, dir.
        *The Choral Ensemble Of Salem College in Concert --
            XTV 62399

        Mississippi University for Women Chapel Choir
        Marilyn Swingle, dir.
        *

        The Sullins Choir
        Leon B. Fleming, Jr., dir.
        Recorded Publications E4QL2071 (1953-1954)

DEBUSSY, Claude (1862-1918)
    La Damoiselle Elue
        Ambrosia Ladies Chorus
        Wyn Morris, cond.
        Peters PLE 021

        Choeur de l'Orchestre de Paris
        Daniel Barenboim, cond.
        Deutsche Gramaphon 2531-263

        Maitrise de la R.T.F.
        Boite a Musique LD 5080

La Damoiselle Elue (continued)
    NBC Symphony & Womens Chorus
    Arturo Toscanini, cond.
    Toscanini Conducts Debussy -- Olympic ATS 1106/1107

    Radcliffe Choral Society (G. Wallace Woodworth)
    Charles Munch, cond.
    RCA Victor LM 1907

    San Francisco Symphony Chorus
    Phillips 6514199

    Stuttgart Radio Womens Chorus
    Pro Art 128

    Theatre des Champs-Elysees Chorus and Orchestra
    Westminster WL 5336

    Women's Chorus of the University of Pennsylvania
    Eugene Ormandy, cond.
    Columbia ML 4075

Nocturnes (Sirenes)
    BBC Women's Chorus
    London Symphony
    Seraphim S-60104

    Berkshire Festival Chorus Women
    P. Monteux, cond.
    Victrola 1027 (3D-VICS-1027)

    Cleveland Symphony Chorus Women
    L. Maazel, cond.
    London STS 15585

    Collegium Musicum Of Amsterdam Womens Chorus
    Concertgebouw Orchestra
    Phillips 9500674

    Czech Philharmonic Women's Chorus
    Josef Veselka, cond.
    Crossroads 22-16-0092; Supraphon SUA ST 50-575

    French National Radio Women's Chorus
    John Barbirolli, cond.
    Angel S-36583; Angel S-37067

    John Alldis Choir
    P. Boulez
    Columbia M 30483

Nocturnes (Sirenes) (continued)
        Oratorio Society Women's Voices
        A. Dorati, cond.
        London CS 6968

        Temple University Women's Chorus
        E. Ormandy, cond.
        Columbia MG 30950

    Reverie
        Peninsula Women's Chorus
        Patricia Hennings, dir.
        *Song of Survival

    Salut Printemp
        Choeur de l'Orchestre de Paris
        Daniel Barenboim, cond.
        Deutsche Gramaphon 2531-263

    We Sing To Spring
        Lyons Township High School Treble Choir
        Lynne Bradley, dir.
        *Bursting Out -- Delta DRS 82M 116

        South Houston Girls Choir
        Sally Schott, dir.
        *Crest Records -- ACD 81-2B

DeCORMIER, Robert (arr.)
    Coulters Candy
        The Aeolian Singers
        Clarie Wall, dir.
        *The Aeolian Singers

    Sometimes I Feel Like A Motherless Child
        East Carolina University Women's Glee Club
        Rhonda Fleming, dir.
        *HIS Recording

DeGOEDE, N. (1915-   )
    Ara vare Gud i hojden (1970)
    Forlossningen ar vunnen (Psalm 50)
    Guds angel kom till herdar i vall (The First Nowell)
    Varldens Fralsare kom har (Psalm 58)
        Brigittasnstrarnasklosterkor
        N. deGoede, dir.
        Rosa Roran Bonitatem -- Proprius PROP 7730

DELLO JOIO, Norman (1913-   )
    A Jubilant Song
        Clovis High School Women's Choir
        Wayne Anderson, dir.
        *Contest Selections 1981

DENVER, John (arr. Philip Lane)
    Annie's Song
        Cheltenham Ladies' College Choir
        Dorothy Dickinson, dir.
        Cantique -- Alpha APS 321

DERING, Richard (1580-1630)
    Above Him Stood The Seraphim
        Westover Glee Club
        Robert Harvey, cond.
        *

    Duo Seraphim Clambant
        Paisley Abbey Choir
        George McPhee, dir.
        In Quires and Places #24 -- Abbey LPB 789

        Tewkesbury Abbey School Choir
        Michael Paterson, dir.
        Tewkesbury Abbey School Choir -- Abbey APS 314

    Gaudent in caelis
        Chapel Choir of the Blue Coat School, Birmingham
        Hugh Shelton, dir.
        Abbey LPB 766

        Choir and School of S. Mary and S. Anne
        Llywela Harris, dir.
        In Quires and Places #5 -- Abbey LPB 668

        Coventry Cathedral Boys Choir
        David Lepine, cond.
        Gloria In Excelsis -- Chapter One CMS 1007

        Leeds Parish Church Choir
        Donald Hunt, cond.
        Abbey LPB 715

        Tewkesbury Abbey School Choir
        Michael Paterson, dir.
        Tewkesbury Abbey School Choir - Abbey APS 314

    O Bone Jesu
        Choir and Schools of S. Mary and S. Anne
        Llywela Harris, dir.
        In Quires And Places #5 -- Abbey LPB 668

        Coventry Cathedral Boys Choir
        David Lepine, cond.
        Gloria In Excelsis -- Chapter One CMS 1007

        Leeds Parish Church Choir
        Donald Hunt, dir.
        Abbey LPB 715

DIAMOND, David (1915-   )
     All In Green Went My Love Riding
          The University Of North Carolina Choir
          Richard Cox, dir.
          *Twentieth Century Compositions for Treble Voices --
               CSS 554

     Young Joseph
          Choir of Mary Baldwin College
          Gordon Page, dir.
          *Richmond Sound Stage 10725

DILASSO, Orlando (SEE: Orlando LASSUS)

DIEMER, Emma Lou (1927-   )
     Alleluia
          Mississippi University for Women Chapel Choir
          Marilyn Swingle, dir.
          *

     Fragments From The Mass
          West Texas State University Chorale
          Hugh Sanders, dir.
          *Golden Crest ATH 5063

     Jesus Lover Of My Soul
          Wheaton College Women's Chorale
          Marry Hopper, cond.
          *Let All The World In Every Corner Sing - WETN 820-50-1

DISTLER, Hugo (1908-1942)
     Der Jahrkreis, Op. 5 (selections for womens voices in
               3-parts) Contents: #6-Macht hoch die Tur;
               #9-Ehre sei Gott in der Hohe; #10-Lobt Gott, ihr
               Christen allzugleich; #14-Jesu deine Passion;
               #17 Erschienen ist der herrlich Tag; #22-Nun
               bitten wir den heiligen Geist; #24-Ein neu Gebot
               gebe ich euch; #36-Der Mensch, vom Weibe geboren;
               #43-Wo Gott zum Haus nit gibt sein Ganst
          Westphalian Kantorei
          Wilhelm Ehmann, cond.
          Musical Heritage Society MHS 3655 (1977)

     Four Songs from the Morike-Chorliederbuch (Erstes liebeslied
               eines Madchens)
          Bemidji State College Concert Choir
          Paul Brandvik, dir.
          Century

     Motets From Der Jahrkreis, Op. 5 (Erschienen ist der herrlich'
               Tag; Mit Freuden Zart; Christ fuhr gen Himmel; Der
               Mensch, vom Weibe geboren; Amen)
          Radcliffe Choral Society
          Beverly Taylor, cond.
          AFKA Records SK 4674

DOWLAND, John (1563-1626)
    Come Again, Sweet Love, Doth Now Invite
        The Aeolian Singers
        Claire Wall, dir.
        *The Impossible Dream Come True

DRECHSLER, Joseph (1782-1852)
    Bruderlein fein (from Der Bauer als Millionar)
        Vienna Choir Boys
        Hans Gilleberger, dir.
        Vienna Choir Boys Serenade -- RCA PRL 1-9034

DRYBURG, Margaret
    The Captive's Hymn (1942)
        Peninsula Women's Chorus
        Patricia Hennings, dir.
        *Song of Survival

DUFAY, Guillaume (1400-1474)
    Magnificat in the Fifth Mode (ed. Richard Cox)
        University Women's Chorus - UNC-G
        William McIver, cond.
        *Crest S-ACDA 80-5B

    Missa Caput
        Girls Chorus Of Gyor
        Miklos Szabo, cond.
        Qualiton LPX 11441

DURUFLE, Maurice (1902-   )
    Tota Pulchra Es (Quatre Motets sur des themes Gregorien)
        The Aeolian Singers
        Claire Wall, dir.
        *The Impossible Dream Come True

        Choir of S. Mary & S. Anne
        Llywela Harris, dir.
        Ave Maria: A Celebration of Carols -- Alpha APS 315

        Lyons Township High School Treble Choir
        Lynne Bradley, dir.
        *(1977) -- Delta DRS 77M 621; Crest NC-ACDA 80-6A

        St. Johns College Choir
        George Guest, cond.
        O Sacrum Convivium -- Argo ZRG 662

        Stephane Caillat Chorale
        Maurice Durufle, cond.
        MHS 1819 (1973)

DUSEK, Frantisek Xaver (1731-1799)
    Nottornos (Allegro; Larghetto; Andantino-Allegretto-
            Andantino)
            Chamber Female Chorus of the Czech Philharmonic Chorus
            Supraphon SUA ST 19665

DUSON, Dede
    And Back Again
            South Houston Girls Choir
            Sally Schott, dir.
            *Crest ACD 81-1B

    In Unison
            Lyons Township High School Treble Choir
            Lynne Bradley, dir.
            *Bursting Out -- Delta DRS 82M 116

    To Those Who See
            South Houston Girls Choir
            Sally Schott, dir.
            *Crest ACD 81-2B

DUTCH CAROL
    King Jesus Hath A Garden
            Philomela
            Susan Ames-Zierman, dir.
            Make We Joy -- PR 001

DVORACEK, Jiri (1928-   )
    Nove Jaros
            Pavel Kuhn, cond.
            Panton 11-0408

DVORAK, Anton (1841-1904)
    Die Birke
            Ensemble Lacnica
            Stefan Klimo, dir.
            Chore -- RCA PRLI 9059

    Humoresque
            Peninsula Women's Chorus
            Patricia Hennings, dir.
            *Song of Survival

    Largo from "New World Symphony"
            Peninsula Women's Chorus
            Patricia Hennings, dir.
            *Song of Survival

ELGAR, Edward (1857-1934)
    Ave Verum, Op. 2 #1
        Choir of the School of St. Mary & St. Anne
        Llywela Harris, dir.
        Day By Day -- Argo ZRG 785

    Doubt Not Thy Father's Care
        Temple Church Choir
        George Thalben-Ball, dir.
        Music From The Temple Church -- PVA 2917-545

ENGLISH (13th c.)
    Alle-Psallite-cum luya
        Wells College Choir
        Crawford R. Thoburn, dir.
        *(1980-81)

ENGLISH CAROL
    A Merry Christmas (Oxford Book Of Carols)
        The Salem Academy Glee Club
        Jean Burroughs, dir.
        *(1978-1979) -- Recorded Publications Z530071

    All Under The Leaves (arr. Imogene Holst)
        Choir of S. Mary & S. Anne
        Llywela Harris, dir.
        Ave Maria: A Celebration of Carols -- Alpha APS 315

    Coventry Carol (arr. Scott)
        Women's Choir of UNC-Greensboro
        Richard Cox, dir.
        *Christmas Concert 1974

    Coventry Carol (arr. Thoburn)
        Wells College Choir
        Crawford R. Thoburn
        *(1980-81)

    Deck The Hall (arr. Erickson)
        Womens Choir of UNC-Greensboro
        Richard Cox, dir.
        *Christmas Concert 1974

    Deck The Halls (in 7/8) (arr. McKelvy)
        University of Virginia Women's Chorus
        Katherine Mitchell, dir.
        *Candlelight Christmas -- 8393

    Ding, Dong Merrily On High
        The Sullins Choir
        Leon B. Fleming, Jr., dir.
        Recorded Publications E4QL2071 (1953-1954)

Gloucestershire Wassail
    University of Virginia Women's Chorus
    Katherine Mitchell, dir.
    *Candlelight Christmas -- 8393

God Rest You Merry Gentlemen (arr. Wilcocks)
    University of Virginia Women's Chorus
    Katherine Mitchell, dir.
    *Candlelight Christmas -- 8393

Greensleeves
    Philomela
    Susan Ames-Zierman, dir.
    Make We Joy -- PR 001

Make We Joy
    Philomela
    Susan Ames-Zierman, dir.
    Make We Joy -- PR 001

O Come All Ye Faithful (arr. Wilcocks)
    University of Virginia Women's Chorus
    Katherine Mitchell, dir.
    *Candlelight Christmas -- 8393

Salutation Carol (Ave Maria) (arr. Imogene Holst)
    Choir of S. Mary & S. Anne.
    Llywela Harris, dir.
    Ave Maria: A Celebration of Carols -- Alpha APS 315

Somerset Wassail
    Philomela
    Susan Ames-Zierman, dir.
    Make We Joy -- PR 001

Wassail Song
    University of Virginia Women's Chorus
    Katherine Mitchell, dir.
    *Candlelight Christmas -- 8393

What Child Is This?
    Smith College Glee Club
    Iva Dee Hiatt, cond.
    College Choirs At Christmas -- Classics Record Library
        10-5573 (Book Of The Month Club)

ENGLISH CAROL (14th c.)
    Nowell, Out Of Your Sleep
        Wells College Choir
        Crawford R. Thoburn, dir.
        *(1980-81)

ENGLUND, Einar (arr.) (1916-   )
    Laksin mina kesayona kaymaan (A Walk In The Summer Night)
        Tapiola Choir
        Erkki Pohjola, dir.
        Sounds of Tapiola -- Columbia 5.E-062-34670

EPSTEIN, David (1930-   )
    Night Voices (1974)
        Boston Boy Choir
        David Epstein, cond.
        Candide CE-31116

ESTEP, Garry
    Praise Ye The Lord
        Cincinnati Boys Choir
        William Dickinson, dir.
        *The Cincinnati All-City Boychoir 1974-75

EVANS-HASTINGS, H. R.
    The Beatitudes
        Bethel College Women's Choir
        Oliver Mogck, dir.
        *(1972)

FALL, Mary (arr.)
    America Medley
        Bethel College Women's Choir
        Mary Fall, cond.
        *1976)

FAURE, Gabriel (1845-1924)
    Ave Verum, Op. 65, #1
        Christ Church Cathedral Choir, Oxford
        Simon Preston, dir.
        Argo ZRG 871

        Gabriel Faure Chorale
        Turnabout TV-S-34486

        Choir of Liverpool Metropolitan Cathedral of Christ
            The King
        Philip Duffay, dir.
        Abbey LPB 816

        The London Oratory Junior Choir
        John Hoban, dir.
        Laetare Jerusalem -- Abbey MVP-782

        Choristers of Worcester Cathedral
        Abbey LPB 764 (1976)

Cantique de Jean Racine
    Cheltenham Ladies' College Choir
    Dorothy Dickinson, dir.
    Cantique -- Alpha APS 321

    Gabriel Faure Chorale
    Turnabout TV-S-34486 (1972)

En Priere
    Gabriel Faure Chorale
    Turnabout TV-S-34486 (1972)

In Paradiseum (Requiem)
    Gabriel Faure Chorale
    Turnabout TV-S-34486

    School Sisters of St. Francis
    Sister Marie Gnader, dir.
    *Rhapsody of Praise (St. Joseph Convent)

Maria Mater Gratiae
    Choir of S. Mary & S. Anne
    Llywela Harris, dir.
    Ave Maria: A Celebration of Carols -- Alpha APS 315

    Gabriel Faure Chorale
    Turnabout TV-S-34486

    The London Oratory Junior Choir
    John Hoban, dir.
    Laetare Jerusalem -- Abbey MVP 782

    Choristers of Worcester Cathedral
    Abbey LPB-764

Messe Basse
    (un-named ensemble)
    MHS 4349

    Gabriel Faure Chorale
    Turnabout 34486

    King's College, Cambridge
    Philip Ledger
    ASD 4234; Angel DS 37918

    Lichfield Cathedral Choir
    Jonathan Rees-Williams, dir.
    Hear My Prayer -- Alpha ACA 516

    Maitrise d'enfants
    Jacques Jouineau, cond.
    Pathe DTX 247

Messe Basse (continued)
St. John's College, Cambridge
George Guest, cond.
O Sacrum Convivium -- Argo ZRG-662

Choristers of Worcester Cathedral
Abbey LPB-764

Pie Jesu (Requiem)
Cincinnati Boys Choir
William Dickinson, dir.
*Cincinnati Boychoir Plays Nashville

Gabriel Faure Chorale
Turnabout TVS 34486

Salve Regina
Choristers of Worcester Cathedral
Abbey LPB 764

Tantum Ergo, Op. 65, #2
Choirs of Bradford Cathedral
Keith Rhodes, dir.
The Choirs of Bradford Cathedral -- Abbey APR 306

Gabriel Faure Chorale
Turnabout 34486

The London Oratory Junior Choir
John Hoban, dir.
Laetare Jerusalem -- Abbey MVP 782

Maitrise d'enfants
Jacques Jouineau, cond.
Pathe DTX 247

University Choir
Richard Cox, dir.
*Christmas Concert 1967 - Robbins Recording 1911-a

FERNSTROM, John (1897-1961)
Concertino for Flute, Women's Chorus and Chamber Orchestra
Op. 52
Stockholm Radio Orchestra & Chorus
Sten Frykberg, cond.
Turnabout S-34498

FESTA, Costanzo (1490-1545)
    Amor che mi consigli?
        Vassar Madrigal Singers
        E. Harold Geer, cond.
        The Italian Madrigals: Ars Nova and the 16th c. --
            Allegro Records ALG 2039

FINE, Irving (1914-1962)
    Alice in Wonderland (Second Series)
            (The Knaves Letter; The White Knight's Song;
            Beautiful Soup)
        Gregg Smith Singers
        Gregg Smith, cond.
        The Choral Music Of Irving Fine -- Composers
            Recording SD 376

    Beautiful Soup (Alice in Wonderland, Set II)
        South Houston Girls Choir
        Sally Schott, dir.
        *Crest ACD-81-2B

FINE, Vivian (1913-)
    Paean (1969)
        Bennington Choral Ensemble with Eastman Brass Ensemble
        Composers Recording CRI SD 260

FINETTI, Giacomo (1605-1631)
    O Maria quae rapis corda hominum
        The London Oratory Junior Choir
        John Hoban, dir.
        Laetare Jerusalem -- Abbey MVP 782

FOSTER, Stephen (1826-1864)
    Nelly Bly (arr. Robinson)
        Women of Mormon Tabernacle Choir
        Richard Condie, cond.
        Beautiful Dreamer -- Comumbia MS 7149

FRACKENPOHL, Arthur P. (1924-)
    Lovers Love The Spring
        Alabama Music Educators All State
        Hugh Thomas, dir.
        *Alabama Music Educators Grant Concert 1978 -- USC
            Sound

FRANCOIS, Claude and Jacques Revaux
    My Way (Comme d'habitude) (arr. Barry Rose)
        St. Paul's Cathedral Boys Choir
        Rejoice -- K-Tel NE-1064

FRANCK, Cesar (1822-1890)
    O Salutaris Hostias
        Worcester Cathedral Choir
        Donald Hunt, dir.
        French Church Music, Vol. I -- Abbey LPB 758

    Panis Angelicus
        Cincinnati BoysChoir
        William Dickinson, dir.
        *Now Gentlemen

        Choir Of Liverpool Metropolitan Cathedral of Christ
            The King
        Philip Duffay, dir.
        Abbey LPB 816

        London Oratory Junior Choir
        John Hoban, dir.
        Abbey MVP 782

FRENCH CAROL
    Angels We Have Heard On High (19th c.)
        Philomela
        Susan Ames-Zierman, dir.
        Make We Joy -- PR 001

    Bring a Torch (arr. Rodney Russell Bennet)
        Women of Robert Shaw Chorus
        Robert Shaw, dir.
        Many Moods Of Christmas -- Telarc DG 100087

    Bring Your Torch (arr. Franz Wasner)
        Women of Mormon Tabernacle Choir
        Richard Condie, dir.
        The Mormon Tabernacle Choir Christmas Celebration --
            Book Of The Month Club 11-6433

    Entre le Boeuf et l'ane gris
        Philomela
        Susan Ames-Zierman, dir.
        Make We Joy -- PR 001

    Jacques, Come Here (arr. Richard Donovan)
        Smith College Glee Club
        Iva Dee Hiatt, cond.
        College Choirs At Christmas -- Book of the Month
            Record 21-6522

    Joseph est bien marie (arr. Richard Donovan)
        Smith College Glee Club
        Iva Dee Hiatt, dir.
        College Choirs At Christmas -- Book Of The Month Record
            21-6522

Qui dirait que Dieu
    Philomela
    Susan Ames-Zierman, dir.
    Make We Joy -- PR 001

FRENCH FOLK SONG
    Gai lon la
        The Aeolian Singers
        Claire Wall, dir.
        *The Impossible Dream Come True

FRIBERG, Carl (1939-   )
    I Climbed The Mountain
        Lyons Township High School Treble Choir
        Lynne Bradley, dir.
        *(1977) -- Delta DRS 77M-621

FRYXELL, Regina (1899-   )
    Psalm 67
        Salem College Choral Ensemble
        Paul W. Peterson, dir.
        *On The Campus and On The Road -- Starr Mount

GAELIC MELODY
    Morning Has Broken
        St. Paul's Cathedral Boys Choir
        K-Tel NE-1064

GALLUS, Jacobus (SEE: Jacob HANDL)

GALUPPI, Baldasarre (1706-1785)
    Dixit Dominus (Psalm 110)
        Lyons Township High School Treble Choir
        Lynne Bradley, dir.
        *(1979) -- Delta DRS-79M-614; #(1976) Century Advent
            LF48-756

    Juravit Dominus (from Dixit Dominus)
        Lyons Township High School Treble Choir
        Lynne Bradley, dir.
        *(1977) -- Delta DRS 77M-621

    Laudate Pueri a due cori
        Lyons Township High School Choir & Women of the
            Roosevelt University Choir
        David Larson, cond.
        *Laudate Pueri Dominimum a due cori -- Delta DRS 78M
            720A

GARDNER, John (1943-   )
    The Holly And The Ivy
        Choir Of Leeds Parish Church
        Donald Hunt, dir.
        Christmas At Leeds Parish Church -- Abbey MVP 756

GARDNER, Kay (1941-   )
     Mermaids
          (un-named performers)
          Emerging -- WWE/Urana Records

GARLAND, Joseph C. (1903-   )
     In The Mood
          The Salem Academy Glee Club
          Jean Burroughs, dir.
          *(1978-1979) -- Recorded Publications Z 530071

GASPARINI, Quirino (1721-1778)
     Adoramus Te
          The Choral Ensemble of Salem College
          Paul Peterson, dir.
          *The Choral Ensemble Of Salem College In Concert --
               XTV 62399

GAUL, Harvey (1881-1945)
     List! The Cherubic Hosts
          The Ladies Triple Trio
          *His Glorious Presence -- Mennonite Hour Recordings
               MHLP 13-ST

GEISLER, John
     High Delights Are In The Sons Of Men
          Salem Academy Glee Club
          Jean Burroughs, dir.
          *(1980-81) -- Recorded Publications Z577041

GEIST, Christian (1640-1711)
     De funere ad vitam
          The Collegium Sagittarii
          Derek McCulloch, dir.
          Oryx EXP 26

GELD, Gary ("Bugs" Bower) (1935-   )
     Walk Him Up The Stairs (Purlie)
          Lyons Township High School Treble Choir
          Lynne Bradley, dir.
          *(1977) -- Delta DRS 77M-621

GERMAN CAROL
     In Dulci Jubilo
          Cheltenham Ladies' College Choir
          Dorothy Dickinson, dir.
          Cantique -- Alpha APS 321

     Lieb Nachtigall, wach auf
          Philomela
          Susan Ames-Zierman, dir.
          Make We Joy -- PR 001

Quem Pastores Laudavere (arr. John Rutter)
     Boys' Choir of St. Mary's Hall, Stonyhurst
     Harry Duckworth, dir.
     Carols from St. Mary's Hall, Stonyhurst -- Alpha APS348

Swiftly Thou The Silver Sky
     The Wells College Choir
     Crawford R. Thoburn
     *

Von Himmel Hoch
     Philomela
     Susan Ames-Zierman, dir.
     Make We Joy -- PR 001

GERSHWIN, George (1898-1937)
  Oh, I Can't Sit Down
     Lyons Township High School Treble Choir
     Lynne Bradley, dir.
     *(1977) -- Delta DRS 77M-621

  Porgy and Bess
     Wheelock College Glee Club
     Leo Collins, dir.
     *Vogts Quality Recording

GIBBONS, Orlando (1583-1625)
  O Lord Increase My Faith (arr. Talmadge)
     Bethel College Women's Choir
     Oliver Mogck, dir.
     *(1972)

GIBBS, C. Armstrong (1889-1960)
  Queen Elizabeth's Song (from A Lyric Garland)
     Choir and School of S. Mary and S. Anne
     Llywela Harris
     In Quires and Places #5 -- Abbey LPB 668

GILBERT, John (1934-   )
  The Lord's Prayer
     Cheltenham Ladies' College Choir
     Dorothy Dickinson, dir.
     Cantique -- Alpha APS 321

GILLESPIE, Haven (1888-1975)
  Santa Claus Is Coming To Town
     Harlem Children's Choir
     Richard Wolfe, cond.
     Book Of The Month -- 11-6562

GIOVANNI DA CICONIA (14th c.)
Una panthera in compagnia de Marte
        Vassar Madrigal Singers
        E. Harold Geer, cond.
        The Italian Madrigal: Ars Nova and the 16th c. --
            Allegro Records alg 3029

GOEMANNE, Noel (1926-   )
Missa Hosanna (Kyrie, Sanctus)
        Miami Boy Choir
        Paul A. Eisenhart, cond.
        *Crest - S-ACDA-80-4B

Rondo For Children
        Miami Boy Choir
        Paul A. Eisenhart, dir.
        *Crest - ACD-81-3B

GOUNOD, Charles (1818-1893)
O Divine Redeemer (arr. Treharne)
        Columbus BoyChoir
        Herbert Huffman, dir.
        Festival of Song -- Decca DL 8106

GRABNER, Herman (1886-1969)
Snow
        The Budapest Children's Choir
        Laszlo Czanyi, cond.
        The Budapest Children's Choir At Carnegie Hall --
            Victor LM 2861

GRANCINI, Michaelangelo (1605-1669)
Dulcis Christe
        The London Oratory Junior Choir
        John Hoban, dir.
        Laetare Jerusalem -- Abbey MVP 782

GRANDI, Alessandro (1580-1630)
Hodie Nobis De Caelo
        Westover Glee Club
        Robert Harvey, cond.
        *

O Sacrum Convivium
        The London Oratory Junior Choir
        John Hoban, dir.
        Laetare Jerusalem -- Abbey MVP 782

GREEK CHRISTMAS, A
(Carols & Christmas music in English & Greek)
        Eusebia Choir
        Helen Economopolou, dir.
        Capitol DT-10489

GREENE, Maurice (1695-1775) (arr. Ley)
    I Will Lay Me Down In Peace (from O God Of My Righteousness)
        Litchfield Cathedral Choir
        Anthony Greening, dir.
        Ascension -- Abbey LPB 690

    Thou Visitest The Earth
        Chapel Choir of the Blue-Coat School, Birmingham
        Hugh Shelton, dir.
        Abbey LPB 645

GREENING (arr.)
    Friends
        Lyons Township High School Treble Choir
        Lynne Bradley, dir.
        *Friends -- Delta DRS-81M-105

GREER, C. H. (arr.)
    Four Polish Carols
        The Choral Ensemble of Salem College
        Paul Peterson, dir.
        *The Choral Ensemble of Salem College in Concert -
            XTV62399

GREGORIAN CHANT
    Chants from Lauds and Vespers
        Nuns' Choir of the Abbey of Notre-Dame D'Argentan
        Puer Natus Est Nobis -- Alpha ACA 510

    (Selection: Rosa rorans boitatem; Alma Redemptoris Mater;
            Salve Regina; Benedicamus Domino)
        Brigittasnstrarnas klosterkor
        N. deGoede, dir.
        Rosa Rorans Bonitatem -- Proprius PROP 7730

    (Selections)
        The Choir Of The Sisters Of Divine Providence
        Sister M. Alvin, cond.
        Gregorian Institute Of America CA 8 (1964)

    (Selections: Conditor alme siderum; Vox clara; Christe
            Redemptor; Hostis Herodes; Audi benigne conditor;
            Jam Christe; Vexilla Regis; Crux Fidelis; Ave
            Maris Stella; O Gloriosa Domina; Tibi Christe;
            Orbis Patrator; Ut Queant Laxis; Jam Bone Pastor;
            Jesu Cornoa Virginum; Christe Redemptor; Angularis
            Fundamentum)
        Choir of Nuns of the Abbey of Notre Dame d'Argentan
        Peters PLE 081

    (Selections)
        Choir Of Nuns At Tyburn Convent
        David Read, cond.
        Coimbra CCO73

Easter Day (Invitatory, Hymn, Introit, Kyrie, Gloria,
        Gradual, Alleluia, Sequence, Offertory, Sanctus,
        Agnus Dei, Communion)
    Nins' Choir of the Abbey of Notre-Dame d'Argentan
    Schola Saint-Gregorie du Mans
    Alleluia -- Alpha ACA 525

Easter Vigil (Lumen Christi, Exsultet, Canticum, Alleluia,
        Litany, Antiphon, Offertory, Communion)
    Nuns' Choir of the Abbey of Notre-Dame d'Argentan
    Schola Saint-Gregoire du Mans
    Alleluia -- Alpha ACA 525

The Feast Of St. Michael: The Mass and The Office
    Choir Of Nuns Of Abbey Of Notre Dame d'Argentan
    Peters International PLE 006

Mass Of The Day
    Nuns' Choir of the Abbey of Notre-Dame D'Argentan
    Puer Natus Est Nobis -- Alpha ACA 510

Mass For Easter Sunday
    Schola Antiqua (women)
    R. John Blackley, dir.
    Tenth Century Liturgical Chant -- Nonesuch H-71348

Midnight Mass Of Christmas
    Nuns' Choir of the Abbey of Notre-Dame D'Argentan
    Puer Natus Est Nobis -- Alpha ACA 510

GREYSON
    Mother, I Will Have A Husband
        New Mexico All State Girls' Choir
        John D. Raymond, dir.
        *New Mexico Music Educators Association - 1968 --
            Century Stereo 29256

GREUBER, Franz (1787-1863)
    Silent Night
        The Salem Academy Glee Club
        Jean Burroughs, dir.
        *(1980-81) -- Recorded Publications Z-577041

    Silent Night, Holy Night (arr. & orch. Mark Blatchly)
        St. Paul's Cathedral Boys Choir
        Rejoice -- K-Tel NE 1064

GRIEG, Edvard (1843-1907)
    God's Peace Is Peace Eternal
        Mississippi University For Women Chapel Choir
        Marilyn Swingle, dir.
        *

    Morning from "Peer Gynt Suite"
        Peninsula Women's Chorus
        Patricia Hennings, dir.
        *Song of Survival

GRUNDTVIG, Svend (1824-1883)
    Contents: Morgenstund hr guld i mund; Den signede dag; Giv
            mig, Gud en salmetunge; Skyerne grane; Alle mine
            kinder skal vaere hos dig; Du, som gar ud fra
            den levende Gud; Vaer lovet, du, som, evig
            vagner; Nu ringer alle klokker mod sky; Frelseren
            er mig en hyrde god; Den store mester kommer;
            Til Himlene raekker din miskundhed, Gud
        Danish Radio Girls' Choir
        F. Wagner, dir.
        EG TVED EGT LP 5

GUARNIERI, Camargo (1907-   )
    Suite Vila Rica (3 Afro-Brazalia Poems)
        Associacao de Canto Carol
        C. Guarnieri, cond.
        Festa IG 79.019 (1969)

GUERRERO, Francisco (1528-1599)
    The Kings Follow The Star
        The University Choir
        Richard Cox, dir.
        *Christmas Concert 1963 -- CSS 275-1530A

GURIDI, Jesus (1896-1961)
    Arno Nun Hun Huntariu (#2 in Asi Cantan Los Chicos)
        Sociedad coral de Bilbao & Orchestra
        Urbano Ruiz Laorden, cond.
        Columbia SCLL 14090 (1972)

HADLEY, Patrick (1899-1973)
    I Sing Of A Maiden
        Alexandra Choir
        David Hill, cond.
        We Wish You A Merry Christmas -- Alpha ACA 520

        Kings College, Cambridge
        Philip Ledger, cond.
        Carols for Christmas Eve -- EMI CSD-3774

        Kings College, Cambridge
        David Willcocks, dir.
        A Procession With Carols for Advent Season -- Argo
            ZRG 45240

        Leeds Parish Church
        Donald Hunt, dir.
        Christmas At Leeds Parish Church -- Abbey MVP 756

        Pueri Sanctae Mariae (The Boys' Choir of St. Mary's
            Hall, Stonyhurst)
        Harry Duckworth, dir.
        Carols from St. Mary's Hall, Stonyhurst -- Alpha
            APS 348

        St. Luke's Chapel Choir
        Clifford Clark, dir.
        Sing Joyfully -- Lyrichord LLST-7249

        St. Mary's Stonyhurst
        Harry Duckworth, dir.
        Carols from St. Mary's Stonyhurst -- Alpha APS 348

        Southend Boys Choir
        Michael Crabb, dir.
        Christmas Music -- Vista VPS 1068

HAGEMANN, Philip
    Mass
        Rockland County Choral Society
        Philip Hagemann, cond.
        *Crest E-ACDA-80-6B

HAMLISCH, Marvin (1944-   )
    The Way We Were
        The Aeolian Singers
        Claire Wall, dir.
        *The Impossible Dream Come True

HANDEL, G. F. (1685-1759)
    Awake The Trumpet's Lofty Sound (Samson) (arr. Tillinghast)
        Bethel College Women's Choir
        Mary Fall, cond.
        *(1976)

        Mississippi University for Women Chapel Choir
        Marilyn Swingle, dir.
        *

    Daughters of Sion
        The Tapiola Choir
        Erkki Pohjola, cond.
        Tapiolan Joulu 2 -- Qualiton BIS LP 132

    Hallelujah, Amen
        Bethel College Women's Choir
        Oliver Mogck, dir.
        *(Gold Cover)

    How Excellent Thy Name, Hallelujah
        Bethel College Women's Choir
        Mary Fall, cond.
        *(1979)

    How Excellent Thy Name, Hallelujah (arr. Tillinghast)
        Bethel College Women's Choir
        Oliver Mogck, dir.
        *(1972)

    Let The Bright Seraphim
        Choristers of Worcester Cathedral
        Christopher Robinson, dir.
        Music from Worcester Cathedral -- Abbey LPB 611

    O Lovely Peace (from Judas Maccabaeus)
        The Choir of the Parish Church of St. Peter, Leeds
        Donald Hunt
        In Quires and Places -- Abbey LPB 686

    Oh Had I Jubal's Lyre
        Chapel Choir of the Blue Coat School, Birmingham
        Hugh Shelton, dir.
        Abbey LPB 766

HANDL, Jacob (1551-1591)
    Benedictus (ed. McCray)
        Lyons Township High School Treble Choir
        Lynne Bradley, dir.
        *Friends -- Delta-81M-105

Pueri Concinite
Hungarian Radio Children's Choir
Botka & Csanyi, conds.
Hungaroton SLPX 12163

The University Choir
Richard Cox, dir.
*Christmas Concert 1965 -- Copeland CSS 573-2103

Wells College Choir
Crawford R. Thoburn, dir.
*(1980-1981)

Replenti Sunt
Lyons Township High School Treble Choir
Lynne Bradley, dir.
*(1976)

HANNIKAINEN, Pekka Juhani (1854-1924)
Sleep My Child, Sleep
The Tapiola Choir
Erkki Pohjola, cond.
Songs Of Finland -- Qualiton BIS LP-94

Summer Twilight
The Tapiola Choir
Erkki Pohjola, cond.
Songs Of Finland -- Qualiton BIS LP-94

HANSON, Howard (1896-1981)
How Excellent Thy Name
Lyons Township High School Treble Choir
Lynne Bradley, cond.
*(1975)

South Houston Girls Choir
Sally Schott, dir.
*Crest -- ACD-81-2B

HANUS, Jan (1915-   )
The Czech Year, Op. 24
Jan Kuhn Children's Choir and Chamber Ensemble of the
Czech Philharmonic Orchestra
Serenus 12047

HARRIS, William H. (1883-1973)
Behold Now Praise The Lord
Boys of St. George's Chapel, Windsor
Sidney Campbell, cond.
Five Centuries At St. Georges -- Argo ZRG 789

King Of Glory, King Of Peace
Llandaff Cathedral Choir
Michael Smith, cond.
Alpha APS 307

HARRISTON, Jester (arr.)
    Poor Man Lazarus
        Alabama Music Educators All State
        Hugh Thomas, dir.
        *Alabama Music Educators Association 1978 -- USC Sound

HASSE, Johann Adolf (1699-1783)
    Miserere (Misere; Benigne fac)
        Lyons Township High School Treble Choir
        Lynne Bradley, dir.
        *Patterns in Music -- Delta DRS 72-139A

    Miserere in D Minor (Psalm 51)
        Radcliffe Choral Society
        Beverly Taylor
        AFKA Records SK 4672

HASSLER, Hans Leo (1562-1612)
    Cantate Domino
        Agnes Scott College Glee Club
        Richard Hensel, dir.
        *(Spring Concert 1964)

        Clovis High School Women's Choir
        Wayne Anderson, dir.
        *Contest Selections 1981

        Mississippi University for Women Chapel Choir
        Marilyn Swingle, dir.
        *

        Salem College Choral Ensemble
        Paul W. Paterson, dir.
        *On The Campus and On The Road -- CM LP 1006

HATTORI, Koh-ichi
    Divertimento for 12 Voices & 2 Celli (1975)
        Echo Elegante
        Koh-ichi Hattori, cond.
        Japanese Composers -- The Japanese Federation of
            Composers JFC 7609

HAYDN, Franz Joseph (1732-1809)
    Canons (SEE: The Ten Commandments)

    Lully, Lullay
        Philomela
        Susan Ames-Zierman, dir.
        Many Butterflies -- RBR 001

    The Ten Commandments (Canons)
        Gyor Girls Choir
        Miklos Szabo, cond.
        Hungaroton SLPD 12373

HAYDN, Michael (1737-1807)
    Anima Nostra (from Offertorium pro Festo S.S. Innocentium)
        Gyor Girls Choir & Gyor Philharmonic
        Miklos Szanbo, cond.
        Hungaroton SLPX 11678

        Vienna Choir Boys
        Hans Gillesberger, cond.
        Christmas Festival -- RCA PRL 1-8020

    De Profundis Tenebrarum (from Sequentia Ad Festum S.P.
        Augustini)
        Gyor Girls Choir & Gyor Philharmonic
        Miklos Szabo, cond.
        Hungaroton SLPX 11678

    Deutsches Hochmat
        Vienna Choir Boys
        Grossmann

    Gradual in D
        Gyor Girls' Chorus & Gyor Philharmonic
        Miklos Szabo, cond.
        Hungaroton LPX 11531

    Gradual in F
        Gyor Girls' Chorus & Gyor Philharmonic
        Miklos Szabo, cond.
        Hungaroton LPX 11531

    Graduale in Festo S.S. Innocentium die Dominica (Alleluia.
        Laudate pueri Dominum)
        Girls Choir of Gyor
        Miklos Szabo, cond.
        Budapest FX 12301

    Graduale in Festo S.S. Innocentium extra Dominicam
        Girls Choir of Gyor
        Miklos Szabo, cond.
        Budapest FX 12301

    Laudate Pueri Dominum
        The Salem Academy Glee Club
        Jean Burroughs, dir.
        *(1980-81) -- Recorded Publicatios Z 477041

    Missa Sancti Aloysii
        Gyor Girls Choir & Gyor Philharmonic
        Miklos Szabo, cond.
        Hungaroton SLPX 11678

Offertorium pro festo cuiuscunque S'tae Virginis et Martyris
    Gyor Girls Choir
    Miklos Szabo, dir.
    Hungaroton SLPX 11678

Vespers in Festo
    Gyor Girls Chorus & Gyor Philharmonic
    Miklos Szabo, cond.
    Hungaroton LPX 11531

Vespers In Festo S.S. Innocentium
    Girls Choir of Gyor
    Miklos Szabo, cond.
    Budapest FX 12301

HEAD, Michael (1900-   )
    The Little Road To Bethlehem
        Pueri Sanctae Mariae (The Boys' Choir of St. Mary's
            Hall, Stonyhurst)
        Harry Duckworth, dir.
        Carols from St. Mary's Hall, Stonyhurst -- Alpha
            APS 348

HEIDEN, Bernhard (b. 1910)
    Riddles by Jonathan Swift (The Moon, Snow, A Circle, A Pair
        of Dice, Time)
        The University of Southern California Dorians
        Michael Ingham, cond.
        *A Program of Music for Women's Voices from the 20th
            Century -- AEA 1094

HEMINGWAY, Roger (1951-   )
    Magnificat and Nunc Dimittis
        Choristers of Worcester Cathedral
        Abbey LPB 764

HENNAGIN, Michael (1936-   )
    The Unknown
        University of Georgia Women's Glee Club
        Ann Jones, cond.
        *Crest S-ACDA-80-3A

HENRY VIII (attributed to)
    Green Grow'th The Holly
        Philomela
        Susan Ames-Zierman, dir.
        Make We Joy -- PR 001

HENSEL, Richard (arr.) (1926-   )
    O Dear What Can The Matter Be
        Agnes Scott College Glee Club
        Richard Hensel, dir.
        *(Spring Concert 1964)

    On Top Of Old Smoky
        Agnes Scott College Glee Club
        Richard Hensel, dir.
        *(Spring Concert 1964)

HENZE, Hans Werner (1926-   )
    Wiegenlied der Mutter Gottes
        Finchley Children's Music Group
        Richard Andrews, cond.
        Decca LC-0171

HILDEGARD OF BINGEN (1098-1179)
    Kyrie
        Women's Voices Of The Schola Cantorum, University of
            Arkansas
        Jack Groh, cond.
        Music For The Mass By Nun Composers -- Leonarda
            LPI 115

HINDEMITH, Paul (1895-1963)
    A Sound Of Music
        The University Of North Carolina Choir
        Richard Cox, dir.
        *Twentieth Century Compositions For Treble Voices --
            CSS 554

HOLST, Gustav (1874-1934)
    Ave Maria, Op. 9b
        Purcell Singers
        Imogene Holst, cond.
        Songs and Part Songs -- Argo ZRG 512

        University of North Carolina Choir
        Richard Cox, dir.
        *Twentieth Century Compositions for Treble Voices --
            CSS 554

        University Treble Choir (Illinois State University)
        Donald Armstrong, cond.
        *

    Canons For Equal Voices (Contents: If You Love Songs;
        Lovely Venus; The Fields Of Sorrow; David's
        Lament for Jonathan; Evening On The Moselle; If
        'twere the Time Of Lillies)
        The Purcell Singers
        Imogene Holst, cond.
        Argo -- ZRG 5497

Choral Hymns from the Rig Veda, Op. 26, #2
    St. Pauls Cathedral Choir
    Sir Charles Groves, cond.
    Angel SQ 37455 (1978)

Choral Hymns from the Rig Veda Op. 26, #3 (Hymn To The
        Dawn; Hymn To The Waters; Hymn To The Vena)
    Lyons Township High School Treble Choir
    Lynne Bradley, dir.
    *Patterns In Music -- Delta DRS 74-139A

Choral Hymns from the Rig Veda, Op. #3 (Hymn To The Dawn;
        Hymn To The Waters; Hymn To Vena; Hymn To The
        Travellers)
    Women of The Purcell Singers
    Imogene Holst, cond.
    Argo ZNF-6 (1966)

Lord, Who Hast Made Us For Thine Own (Psalm 148 paraphrase)
    Choir And School of S. Mary and S. Anne
    Llywela Harris,
    In Quires And Places #5 -- Abbey LPB 668

    Lyons Township High School Treble Choir
    Lynne Bradley, dir.
    *Friends -- Delta DRS 81M-105

The Planets, Op. 32 (Neptune)
    John Alldis Choir
    Phillips 6500072 (Haitinik)

    Ambrosian Singers
    Angel DS 37817; Angel S-36420 (Boult); Angel S-36991
        (Previn)

    Ambrosian Singers
    Phillips 9500.425 (Marriner)

    BBC Women's Chorus
    HMV Treasury HLM 7014; Capitol EMI SG 7196

    Mendelssohn Choir of Philadelphia Womens Voices
    RCA CRL-1-1921

    RIAS Kammerchor & Berlin Philharmonic
    Herbert von Karajan, cond.
    Deutsche Grammophon 400 028-2 (compact disc)

    St. Louis Orchestra & Chorus
    Walter Susskind
    Vox/Turnabout 34598 CT 2153

The Planets, Op. 32 (Neptune) (continued)
  Roger Wagner Chorale Womens Voices & Los Angeles
      Philharmonic
  Leopold Stokowski
  Seraphim S-60175

  Vienna Opera Chorus
  Herbert Von Karajan
  London 41005

Savitri, Op. 25 (Chamber Opera In One Act)
  Purcell Singers
  Imogene Holst, cond.
  Argo ZNF 6

Seven Part Songs, Op. 44 (Contents: Say Who Is This?; O
      Love I Complain; Angel Spirits Of Sleep; When
      First We Met; Sorrow and Joy; Love On My Heart
      From Heaven Fell; Assembled All Ye Maidens)
  Purcell Singers & English Chamber Orchestra
  Imogene Holst, cond.
  Argo ZRG-5495 (1966)

Songs From The Princess (Contents: O Swallow, Swallow;
      Sweet and Low; The Splendor Falls)
  East Carolina University Women's Glee Club
  Rhonda Fleming, dir.
  *HIS Recording

Songs From The Princess (Contents: Sweet and Low; The
      Splendor Falls; Tears Idle Tears; O Swallow,
      Swallow; Now Sleeps The Crimson Petal)
  University Of North Carolina Womens Chorus
  William McIver, cond.
  *Crest S-ACDA-80-5B

Sweet and Low (from Songs From The Princess)
  Lyons Township High School Treble Choir
  Lynne Bradley, dir.
  *(1976)

Two Carols: A Welcome Song; Terly, Terlow
  Purcell Singers
  Imogene Holst, cond.
  Decca ZRG 5497

Two Part Songs: Pastoral; The Swallow Leaves Her Next
  Purcell Singers
  Imogene Holst, cond.
  Argo ZRG 512

HOVHANESS, Alan (1911-   )
    Ave Maria (2nd Movement of Triptych)
        Bay Rund Singers & Bamberg Symphony
        Composers Recording S-221

HOW, Martn
    Day By Day
        Wheaton College Women's Chorale
        Mary Hopper, dir.
        *Let All The World In Every Corner Sing -- WETN 820-50

HOWELLS, Herbert (1892-1983)
    A Maid Peerless
        Thames Chamber Choir
        L. Halsey, cond.
        British Institute Of Recorded Sound M 4679W

HONEGGER, Arthur (1892-1955)
    Cantique de Paques
        Maitrise d'enfants
        Jacques Jouineau, cond.
        Pathe DTX 247

HUMPERDINCK, E. (1864-1921)
    Prayer From Hansel & Gretel
        Mormon Tabernacle Choir
        Richard Condie, cond.
        Now The Day Is Over -- Columbia MS 7399

HUNGARIAN (Traditional)
    Spring Wind
        The Budapest Childrens Choir
        Laszlo Czanyi, dir.
        The Budapest Children's Choir At Carnegie Hall -- RCA
            LM 2861

HUNTINGTON, Jonathan (1800)
    Hark! Hark! The Herald Angels Sing
        Philomela
        Susan Ames-Zierman, dir.
        Make We Joy -- PR 001

HURD, Michael (1928-   )
    Hip-Hip Horatio
        The South End Boys' Choir
        Michael Crabb, dir.
        Vista VPS 1027

HURFORD, Peter (1930-   )
    Litany Of The Holy Spirit
        Chapel Choir of the Blue-Coat School, Birmingham
        Hugh Shelton, dir.
        Abbey LPB 645

HYMN

    Ave maris stella
        The Boston Camerata
        John Cohen, dir.
        A Medieval Christmas -- Nonesuch H 71315

HYMNS

    Christian Life Medley (When I Survey; Channels Only; So I
            Send You; What If It Were Today)
        Bethel College Women's Chorale
        Oliver Mogck, dir.
        *(1976)

    The Church's One Foundation
        Bethel College Women's Choir
        Mary Fall, cond.
        *(1979)

    Fairest Lord Jesus
        Bethel College Women's Choir
        Mary Fall, cond.
        *(1979)

    Processional Medley (The Church's One Foundation; Fairest
            Lord Jesus; Holy, Holy, Holy)
        Bethel College Women's Choir
        Oliver Mogck, dir.
        *(1972)

    Second Coming Medley (Someday I Shall Know Him; When He
            Shall Come)
        Bethel College Women's Choir
        Oliver Mogck, dir.
        *Gold Cover

HYTREK, S. Theophane
    Canticle of the Creatures
        School Sisters of St. Francis
        Sister Marie Gnader, dir.
        *Rhapsody of Praise (St. Joseph Convent)

    Hymns: Blessing of St. Francis; Canticle of the Creatures;
            Come Let Us Sing To The Lord; Dextera Domini;
            O Holy Banquet; St. Francis Song; Rejoice,
            Daughter of Sion
        Chapel Singers School Sister of St. Francis
        S. Marie Gnader, dir.
        *Come Let Us Sing To The Lord! (Cassette)

IBRIAEV, K.
    Pesnia o Lenine.
    Veselaia gorlea zimniaia pol'ka
        (un-named choir)
        A Birchanskii, cond.
        Four Children's Choruses by 3 Soviet Composers --
            (Russian Recording - copy at Library of Congress)

INGALLS, J.
    The Gift Of Song (Ades)
        Lyons Township High School Treble Choir
        Lynne Bradley, dir.
        *(1975) -- Delta DRS 75-423

IRELAND, John (1879-1962)
    Ex Ore Innocentium
        Choir of the School of St. Mary & St. Anne
        Llywela Harris, dir.
        Day By Day -- Argo ZRG 785

        Norwich Cathedral Choir
        Michael Norris, dir.
        John Ireland And His Contemporaries -- Vista VPS 1084

        York Minster Choir
        Francis Jackson, dir.
        Abbey LPB 695

    Greater Love Hath No Man (arr. Carbaugh)
        Moody Women's Glee Club
        Robert Carbaugh, dir.
        *Moody IV -- Moody Bible Institute

IRISH HYMN
    The King of Love My Shepherd Is
        Philomela
        Susan Ames-Zierman, dir.
        Make We Joy -- PR 001

IRISH MELODY
    Cockles and Mussels
        St. Paul's Cathedral Boys Choir
        Rejoice -- K-Tel NE-1064

IVENSEN, M.
    O Krae latviiskorn
        A Birchanskii, cond.
        Four Children's Choruses by 3 Soviet Composers --
            (Russian Recording - copy at Library of Congress)

IVES, Charles (1874-1954)
    A Christmas Carol
        Women of the Berkely Chamber Singers
        Alden Gilchrist, dir.
        MHS 1240 (1971)

    Duty (1921) (Two Slants)
        Glen Ellyn Children's Chorus
        Doreen Rao, conductor
        *Delta/Stereo DRS 76M 536

    Religion (1920)
        Glen Ellyn Children's Chorus
        Doreen Rao, conductor
        *Delta/Stereo DRS 76M 536

JACKSON, Francis (1917-   )
    Magnificat/Nunc Dimittis in C
        Boys of Chester Cathedral
        Roger Fisher, dir.
        The Choristers of Chester Cathedral at Evensong --
            Vista VAS 2001

JACKSON, Nicholas
    Magnificat/Nunc Dimittis
        St. David's Cathedral Choir
        Nicholas Jackson, dir.
        Alpha APR 301

JACOB, Gordon (1895-   )
    A Goodly Heritage (Contents: Under the Greenwood Tree; The
            Cuckoo; The Rewards of Farming; The Grasshopper;
            Rain After Draught; Autumn; When Icicles Hang By
            The All; To Meadow Evening; Pleasure It Is)
        Agnes Scott Glee Club
        Richard Hensel, dir.
        *Anges Scott College Glee Club Spring Concert 1964

JACOBSON, Betty (arr.)
    Vum Vi Ve Vo (Shaker Tune)
        Bethel College Women's Choir
        Mary Fall, cond.
        *(1976)

JACOPO DA BOLOGNA (14th c.)
    Uselletto selvaggio per stagione
        Vassar Madrigal Singers
        E. Harold Geer, cond.
        The Italian Madrigal: Ars Nova and the 16th c. --
            Allegro Records alg 3029

JACQUES-DALCROZE, Emile (1865-1950)
    Le jeu du feuillu (Suite de chanson de Mai, Op. 43)
        Robert Mermoud, cond.
        Communaute de travail pour la diffusion de la Musique
           Suisse CTS 38

JAMAICAN RUMBA
    Mango Walk (arr. John Hosier)
        Choir and School of S. Mary and S. Anne
        Llywela Harris, dir.
        In Quires and Places, #5 -- Abbey LPB 668

JANACEK, Leos (1854-1928)
    The Diary Of One Who Disappeared (for tenor, contralto,
        female chorus & piano)
        Kuhn Female Choir
        Pavel Kuhn, dir.
        Supraphon 1112-2414

    Hradcany Songs (Three Choruses For Female Voices: 1. Golden
        Street; 2. The Weeping Fountain; 3. Belvedere)
        Czech Philharmonic Chorus
        Josef Veselka, cond.
        Choral Works for Female Voices -- Supraphon 112 1486

        Moravian Women Teachers Chorus
        Bretislav Bakala, cond.
        Supraphon SUA 10352 (1965)

        Moravian Women Teachers Chorus
        Supraphon LPV 475

    Kaspar Rucky
        Czech Philharmonic Chorus
        Josef Veselka, cond.
        Choral Music for Female Voices -- Supraphon 112-1486

    Nonsense Rhymes (Rikadla) (Contents: 1. Introduction; 2. At
        The Beetroot's Wedding; 3. There Is No Time Like
        Spring; 4. Morris Mole Creeps Down The Pathway;
        5. Charlie Trotted Off To Hell; 6. Raggy, Raggy
        Trouser Legs; 7. Franky Diddle Played The Bass
        Fiddle; 8. Our Dog's, Our Dog's; 9. Listen! Hear
        What I Say; 10. The Old Witch Made Things of
        Magic; 11. Ho Ho Cow All Go; 12. Tiny Wee Wife I
        Will Pop You; 13. Granny Crawled Into The Tree;
        14. Nanny Goat Collects The Pears; 15. Gerry Bug
        Beat The Jug; 16. In The Hay's A Smiling Goat;
        17. Vashek Pashek Beat The Drum; 18. Franky Boy,
        Franky, Quick; 19. Bruin Bear Sat On A Tree Trunk)
        Czech Philharmonic Chorus
        Josef Vesekla, cond.
        Choral Music for Female Voices -- Supraphon 112-1486

Wolf's Footprints
      Moravian Women Teacher Chorus
      Supraphon LPV 475

Wolf's Track
      Czech Philharmonic Chorus
      Josef Veselka, cond.
      Choral Music For Female Voices -- Supraphon 112-1486

      Moravian Women Teachers Chorus
      Bretislav Bakala, cond.
      Supraphon SUA 10352 (1965)

JANEQUIN, Clement (1485-1558)
    Ce Moys De May
      Salem Academy Glee Club
      Jean Burroughs, dir.
      *(1980-81) -- Recorded Publications Z 577041

JENEY, Zoltan (1943-   )
    Solitude
      Gyor Girls Chorus
      Miklos Szabo, cond.
      Contemporary Hungarian Female Choirs -- Hungaroton
          SLPX 11764

JEWISH FOLK TUNE (arr. Goldman)
    Ya Ba Bom (There Shall Be Peace)
      Lyons Township High School Treble Choir
      Lynne Bradley, dir.
      *Friends -- DRS 81M 105; also Delta DRS 79M 614

JOHANSSON, Bengt (1914-   )
    Cum essen Parvulus
      The Tapiola Choir
      Erkki Pohjola, dir.
      Sounds of Tapiola -- EMI Columbia 5.E-062-34670

    Pater Noster
      The Tapiola Choir
      Erkki Pohjola, cond.
      Deutsche Gramophon 2530.812

JOHNS, Donald (1922-   )
    O Praise The Lord, All Ye Nations
      Bethel College Women's Choir
      Mary Fall, dir.
      *(1976)

      Lyons Township High School Treble Choir
      Lynne Bradley, dir.
      *(1977) Delta DRS 77M 621

JOLIVET, Andre (1905-1974)
     Suite Liturgique (19420)
          Female Chorus of O.R.T.F.
          Jacques Jouineau, cond.
          MHS 1658 (1973)

JOSEQUIN DES PREZ (1440-1521)
     Ave Maria
          Alabama Music Educators All State
          Hugh Thomas, dir.
          *Alabama Music Educators Association All State 1978 --
               USC Sound Enterprises

KABALEVSKY, Dimitry (1904-   )
     Italaula (Evening Song)
          The Tapiola Choir
          Erkki Pohjola, cond.
          Deutsche Gramophon 2530.812; Sounds of Tapiola --
               Columbia 5.3-062-34670

KAGEL, Mauricio (1931-   )
     1898 (for children's voice & instruments)
          Children of the Hauptschule Peter-Griess-Strasse
          Deutsche Grammophon 2543-007

KALMAR, Laszlo (1931-   )
     Four Madrigals (1. With its breezes, its rivers; 2. How Far
               Away We Are; 3. Uninhabited Stone; 4. Decomposed
               Shreds)
          Gyor Girls Chorus
          Miklos Szabo, cond.
          Contemporary Hungarian Female Choirs -- Hungaroton
               SLPX 11764

KANITZ, Ernest (1894-1978)
     Visions At Twilight
          (un-named women's ensemble)
          Jan Popper, cond.
          Orion ORS 75190 (1975)

KANKAINEN, Jukka
     Cycle To Poems by Mika Waltari (1. My Hawk; 2. Evening;
               3. Ecstasy)
          The Tapiola Choir
          Erkki Pohjola, cond.
          Finlandia FA 327

     The Steeple Bell
          The Tapiola Choir
          Erkki Pohjola, cond.
          Finlandia FA 327

KARLIN, Frederick James (1936-   )
    Come Saturday Morning
        The Salem Academy Glee Club
        Jean Burroughs, dir.
        *(1980-81) -- Recorded Publications Z577041

KAY, Ulysses (1917-   )
    Christmas Carol
        University Treble Choir (Illinois State University)
        Donald Armstrong, cond.
        *A Choral Christmas

KEEL, Frederich (arr. Bernell W. Hales)
    Lullaby
        Women of Mormon Tabernacle Choir
        Richard Condie, dir.
        The Mormon Tabernacle Choir Christmas Celebration --
            Book of The Month Record 11-6433

KERR, Anita (arr.)
    Broadway Show Stoppers
        Lyons Township High School Treble Choir
        Lynne Bradley, dir.
        *Bursting Out -- Delta DRS 82M 116

KIRKPATRICK, William J. (1838-1921)
    Away In A Manger (arr. Robinson)
        Choir of Worcester Cathedral
        Christopher Robinson, dir.
        Old English Christmas Carols -- Sine Qua Non SQN 7804;
            Carols from Worcester Cathedral MHS 3510

    Away In A Manger (arr. Willcocks)
        Boys' Choir of St. Mary's Hall, Stonyhurst
        Harry Duckworth, dir.
        Pueri Sanctae Mariae -- Alpha APS 322

KLERK, Albert de (1917-   )
    Missa, Mater Sanctae Laetitiae
        Netherlands Chamber Choir
        Felix de Noble, cond.
        Donemus DAVS 6502 (1965)

KNAB, Armin (1881-1954)
    Sonnenlied (The Swan)
        Obernkirchen Children's Choir
        Edith Moeller, cond.
        Songs and a Wonderful Story -- Angel 35684

KNIGHT, Gerald (1908-   )
    Christ Whose Glory Fills The Skies
        Chapel Choir of the Blue-Coat School, Birmingham
        Hugh Shelton, dir.
        Abbey LPB 645

KOCSAR, Miklos (1933-   )
    Music of the Seasons (Contents: 1. I Hear The Dear Noise
            Stirring; 2. Rejoice My Heart; 3. Tempest; 4. Hot
            Spell; 5. In Early Autumn; 6. Splendid Fading;
            7. Howling; 8. Winter Fog)
        Gyor Girls Chorus
        Miklos Szabo, cond.
        Contemporary Hungarian Female Choirs -- Hungaroton
            SLPX 11764

KODALY, Zoltan (1882-1967)
    Angels and Shepherd (1935)
        Columbus BoyChoir
        Donald Hanson, cond.
        The Columbus BoyChoir Performs Zoltan Kodaly -- CBP
            Records CBP 675

        Kodaly Chorus of the Klara Leowey Secondary School
        Ilona Andor, cond.
        Choral Music II -- Hungaroton LPX 11345

        Kodaly Girls Choir
        Ilona Andor, cond.
        Hungarian Songs -- Angel S 36334

        Kodaly Girls Chorus of Budapest
        Ilona Andor, cond.
        Children's and Female Choruses -- Hungaroton SLPX 1292

        University TrebleChoir (Illinois State University)
        Donald Armstrong, cond.
        *A Choral Christmas

        Vienna Choir Boys
        Hans Gillesberger, cond.
        Christmas Festival -- RCA PRL-18020

    Ave Maria
        Budapest Children's Choir
        Laszlo Czanyi, cond.
        The Budapest Children's Choir at Carnegie Hall --
            Victor LM 2861 (1966)

        Cincinnati BoysChoir
        William Dickinson, dir.
        *The Cincinnati All-City Boychoir

        East Carolina University Women's Glee Club
        Rhonda Fleming, dir.
        *HIS Recording

Ave Maria (continued)
    Zoltan Kodaly Childrens Chorus
    Ilona Andor, cond.
    Choral Works Vol. I -- Hungaroton LPX 1259

    Mexican Children's Choir
    Los Ninos Cantores de Puebla -- Classic Pick 70-114

    Shenandoah Chorus
    Robert McSpadden, cond.
    *Festival of Music 1966 -- Custom Stereo V25575-3

    The Tapiola Choir
    Erkki Pohjola, cond.
    Sounds of Tapiola -- Columbia 5.E-062-34670

The Bells
    Zoltan Kodaly Chorus of Klara Leowey Secondary School
    Ilona Andor, cond.
    Choral Works #4 -- Hungaroton SLPX 11409

Bicinia Hungarica (The True Age; Song of the Thrush; The
        The River Flows; On The Edge Of The Ditch)
    Kodaly Chorus of the Klara Leowey Secondary School
    Ilona Andor, cond.
    Choral Music I -- Hungaroton LPX 11315

Birthday Greeting (1931)
    Kodaly Choir of the Klara Leowey Secondary School
    Ilona Andor, cond.
    Choral Music II -- Hungaroton LPX 11315

Cease Your Bitter Weeping
    Columbus BoyChoir
    Donald Hanson, cond.
    The Columbus BoyChoir Performs Zoltan Kodaly -- CBP
        Records CBP 675

    Zoltan Kodaly Girls Chorus
    Hungaroton SLPX 11612

Choral Works, Volume I
    Kodaly Children's Choir
    Ilona Andor, cond.
    Qualiton LPX 1259

Choral Works, Volume II (Childrens Choruses - 1925-1963)
    Kodaly Chorus of Klara Leowey Secondary School
    Ilona Andor, cond.
    Qualiton SLPX 11315

Choral Works, Volume IV (Children and Female Choruses)
    Kodaly Chorus of the Klara Leowey Secondary School
    Ilona Andor, cond.
    Qualiton SLPX 11409

Choral Works, Volume V (2-part Singing Exercises)
    Budapest-Kodaly Girls Choir
    Ilona Andor, conductor
    Hungaroton LPX 11469

Christmas Shepherd's Dance
    Zoltan Kodaly Chorus of Klara Leowey Secondary School
    Ilona Andor, cond.
    Choral Works IV -- Qualiton SLPX 11409

Christmas Song
    Columbus BoyChoir
    Donald Hanson, cond.
    The Columbus BoyChoir Performs Zoltan Kodaly --
        CBP Records CBP 675

Dancing Song (1929)
    Kodaly Girls Choir
    Ilona Andor, cond.
    Hungarian Songs - Angel S-36334

    Kodaly Girls Chorus of Budapest
    Ilona Andor, cond.
    Children's and Female Choruses -- Hungaroton SLPX
        12492

    Kodaly Chorus of Klara Leowey Secondary School
    Ilona Andor, cond.
    Choral Music IV -- Qualiton SLPX 11409

    Wheaton College Women's Chorale
    Mary Hopper, cond.
    *Let All The World In Every Corner Sing -- WETN 820-501

Deaf Boatman, The (1928)
    Columbus BoyChoir
    Donald Hanson, cond.
    The Columbus BoyChoir Performs Zoltan Kodaly -- CBP
        Records CBP 675

    Kodaly Chorus of the Klara Leowey Secondary School
    Ilona Andor, cond.
    Choral Music IV -- Qualiton SLPX 11409

    Kodaly Girls Chorus of Budapest
    Ilona Andor, cond.
    Children's and Female Choruses -- Hungaroton SLPX 12492

Deceiving Song
    Kodaly Choir of Debrecen
    Gyorgy Gulyas, cond.
    Qualiton LPX 1211 (1964)

Do Not Despair (1939)
    Zoltan Kodaly Girls Chorus
    Ilona Andor, cond.
    Choral Music VII -- Hungaroton LPX 11612

Epiphany (1933)
    Columbus BoyChoir
    Donald Hanson, cond.
    The Columbus BoyChoir Performs Zoltan Kodaly -- CBP
        Records CBP 675

    Kodaly Zoltan Girls Chorus
    Hungaroton SLPX 11612

Evening Song (Iltalaula) (1938)
    Columbus BoyChoir
    Donald Hanson, cond.
    The Columbus BoyChoir Performs Zoltan Kodaly -- CBP
        Records CBP 675

    Hungarian Radio Children's Choir
    Botka & Csanyi, conds.
    Hungaroton SLPX 12163

    Kodaly Choir of The Klara Leowey Secondary School
    Ilona Andor, cond.
    Choral Music II -- Hungaroton LPX 11315

    The Tapiola Choir
    Erkki Pohjola, cond.
    Deutsche Gramophon 2530.812

Fancy (from Shakespeare's Merchant of Venice, Act III,
        Scene 2)
    The Columbus BoyChoir
    Donald Hanson, cond.
    The Columbus BoyChoir Performs Zoltan Kodaly -- CBP
        Records CBP 675

    Kodaly Girls Choir
    Ilona Andor, cond.
    Hungarian Songs -- Angel S-36334

    Zoltan Kodaly Children's Chorus
    Ilona Andor, cond.
    Choral Works I -- Hungaroton LPX 1259

The Foal (1937)
    Zoltan Kodaly Chorus of Klara Leowey Secondary School
    Ilona Andor, cond.
    Choral Music IV -- Qualiton SLPX 11409

Four Italian Madrigals (1. Chi vuol veder; 2. Fior Scoloriti;
        3. Chi d'amor sente; 4. Fuor de la bella caiba)
    Kodaly Zoltan Children's Chorus
    Ilona Andor, cond.
    Choral Works I -- Hungaroton LPX 1259

    Kodaly Girls Chorus of Budapest
    Ilona Andor, cond.
    Children's and Female Choruses -- Hungaroton SLPX
        12492

Gay Song Of The Shepherd
    The Budapest Children's Choir
    Laszlo Czanyi, cond.
    The Budapest Children's Choir at Carnegie Hall --
        Victor LM 2861 (1966)

Gee Up, My Horse (1938)
    Zoltan Kodaly Chorus of Klara Leowey Secondary School
    Ilona Andor, cond.
    Choral Music IV -- Qualiton SLPX 11409

God's Blacksmith (1928)
    Zoltan Kodaly Chorus of Klara Leowey Secondary School
    Ilona Andor, cond.
    Choral Music IV -- Qualiton SLPX 11409

    Kodaly Girls Chorus of Budapest
    Ilona Andor, cond.
    Children's and Female Choruses -- Hungaroton SLPX
        12492

Gopher Hunting (1954)
    Kodaly Choir of the Klara Leowey Secondary School
    Ilona Andor, cond.
    Choral Music II -- Hungaroton LPX 11315

Gipsey Lament
    The Columbus BoyChoir
    Donald Hanson, cond.
    The Columbus BoyChoir Performs Zoltan Kodaly --
        CBP Records CBP

Grow Tresses
    Kodaly Girls Chorus of Budapest
    Ilona Andor, cond.
    Children's and Female Choruses -- Hungaroton SLPX
        12492

The Gypsy
    Kodaly Girls Choir
    Ilona Andor, cond.
    Hungarian Songs -- Angel S-36334

Hair Growing (1937)
    Zoltan Kodaly Chorus of Klara Leowey Secondary School
    Ilona Andor, cond.
    Choral Music IV -- Qualiton SLPX 11409

The Hawk
    Zoltan Kodaly Chorus of Klara Leowey Secondary School
    Ilona Andor, cond.
    Choral Music IV -- Qualiton SLPX 11409

Hey, Ho (1938)
    Kodaly Choir of the Klara Leowey Secondary School
    Ilona Andor, cond.
    Choral Music II -- Hungaroton LPX 11315

Honey, Honey, Honey (1958)
    Kodaly Choir of the Klara Leowey Secondary School
    Ilona Andor, cond.
    Choral Music II -- Hungaroton LPX 11315

I Am An Orphan (1953)
    Kodaly Choir of the Klara Leowey Secondary School
    Ilona Andor, cond.
    Choral Music II -- Hungaroton LPX 11315

I'm Dying, I'm Dying
    Zoltan Kodaly Children Chorus
    Ilona Andor, cond.
    Choral Music I -- Hungaroton LPX 1259

In The Green Forest (1936)
    Budapest Children's Choir
    Laszlo Czanyi, cond.
    The Budapest Children's Choir at Carnegie Hall --
        Victor LM 2861 (1966)

    Hungarian Radio Children's Chorus
    Botka & Cxanyi, conds.
    Hungaroton SLPX 12163

    Zoltan Kodaly Chorus of Klara Leowey Secondary School
    Ilona Andor, cond.
    Choral Music IV -- Qualiton SLPX 11409

    Kodaly Girls Chorus of Budapest
    Ilona Andor, cond.
    Children's and Female Choruses -- Hungaroton SLPX
        12492

Jesus Appears
    Zoltan Kodaly Chorus of Klara Leowey Secondary School
    Ilona Andor, cond.
    Choral Music IV -- Qualiton SLPX 11409

Katalinka
    Zoltan Kodaly Chorus of Klara Leowey Secondary School
    Ilona Andor, cond.
    Choral Music IV -- Qualiton SLPX 11409

King Ladislaus' Men
    Kodaly Girls Choir
    Ilona Andor, cond.
    Hungarian Songs -- Angel S-36334

    Kodaly Girls Chorus of Budapest
    Ilona Andor, cond.
    Children's and Female Choruses -- Hungaroton
        SLPX 12492

Lads of Harasztos (1961)
    Kodaly Choir of the Klara Leowey Secondary School
    Ilona Andor, cond.
    Choral Music II -- Hungaroton LPX 11315

Ladybird
    Columbus BoyChoir
    Donald Hanson, cond.
    The Columbus BoyChoir Performs Zoltan Kodaly --
        CBP Records CBP 675

    Wheaton College Women's Chorale
    Mary Hopper, dir.
    *Let All The World In Every Corner Sing -- WETN 820-50

Laszlo Lengyel
    Kodaly Chorus of the Klara Leowey Secondary School
    Ilona Andor, cond.
    Choral Music II -- Hungaroton LPX 11315

Little Rabbit
    Zoltan Kodaly Chorus of Klara Leowey Secondary School
    Ilona Andor, cond.
    Choral Music IV -- Qualiton SLPX 11409

The Mole Is To Marry (1958)
    Kodaly Choir of the Klara Leowey Secondary School
    Ilona Andor, cond.
    Choral Music II -- Hungaroton LPX 11315

Mountain Nights
    Columbus BoyChoir
    Donald Hanson, cond.
    The Columbus BoyChoir performs Zoltan Kodaly --
        CBP Records CBP 675

    Kodaly Girls Choir
    Ilona Andor, cond.
    Hungarian Songs -- Angel S-36334

    Kodaly Choir of Debrecen
    Gyorgy Gulyas, cond.
    Qualiton LPX 1211 (1964)

Mountain Nights, #1
    St. Paul's Choir
    Christopher Dearnly, dir.
    Son et Lumiere at St. Paul's -- Pye NSPL 18286

Mountain Nights, #4
    Kodaly Girls Chorus of Budapest
    Ilona Andor, cond.
    Children's and Female Choruses -- Hungaroton
        SLPX 12492

Mountain Nights, #5 (1962)
    Kodaly Childrens Chorus
    Ilona Andor, cond.
    Choral Works I -- Qualiton LPX 1259

New Year's Greeting (1925)
    Kodaly Chorus of the Klara Leowey Secondary School
    Ilona Andor, cond.
    Choral Works II -- Hungaroton LPX 11315

Nights In The Mountains I-V
    Zoltan Kodaly Chorus of the Klara Leowey Secondary
        School
    Ilona Andor, cond.
    Choral Music IV -- Qualiton SLPX 11409

Orphan Am I
    Kodaly Girls Chorus of Budapest
    Ilona Andor, cond.
    Children's and Female Choruses -- Hungaroton
        SLPX 12492

Peace Song (1925)
    Kodaly Chorus of the Klara Leowey Secondary School
    Ilona Andor, cond.
    Choral Music II -- Hungaroton LPX 11315

Psalm 150
     Columbus BoyChoir
     Donald Hanson, cond.
     The Columbus BoyChoir Performs Zoltan Kodaly --
         CBP Records CBP 675

     Zoltan Kodaly Children Chorus
     Ilona Andor, cond.
     Choral Works I -- Hungaroton LPX 1259

     Kodaly Girls Choir
     Ilona Andor, cond.
     Hungarian Songs -- Angel S 36334

     Kodaly Girls Chorus of Budapest
     Ilona Andor, cond.
     Children's and Female Choruses -- Hungaroton
         SLPX 12492

Quattro madrigali
     Hanover Women's Chorus
     Ludwig Rutt, cond.
     Camerata CMS 30.068 LPT

St. Gregory's Day (1926)
     Kodaly Chorus of the Klara Leowey Secondary School
     Ilona Andor, cond.
     Choral Works II -- Hungaroton LPX 11315

See The Gipsies
     Columbus BoyChoir
     Donald Hanson, cond.
     The Columbus BoyChoir Performs Zoltan Kodaly --
         CBP Records CBP 675

     Kodaly Girls Choir
     Ilona Andor, cond.
     Angel S-36334

     Kodaly Girls Chorus of Budapest
     Ilona Andor, cond.
     Children's and Female Choruses -- Hungaroton
         SLPX 12492

See The Gypsey Munching Cheese (1925)
     Zoltan Kodaly Chorus of Klara Leowey Secondary School
     Ilona Andor, cond.
     Choral Music IV -- Qualiton SLPX 11409

Shepherd's Christmas Dance
     Kodaly Girls Chorus of Budapest
     Ilona Andor, cond.
     Children's and Female Choruses -- Hungaroton SLPX 12492

Singing Youth (1962)
      Kodaly Choir of the Klara Leowey Secondary School
      Ilona Andor, cond.
      Choral Music II -- Hungaroton LPX 11315

Straw Guy (1925)
      Kodaly Chorus of the Klara Leowey Secondary School
      Ilona Andor, cond.
      Choral Works II -- Hungaroton LPX 11315

      Kodaly Girls Chorus of Budapest
      Ilona Andor, cond.
      Children's and Female Choruses -- Hungaroton SLPX 12492

Stork Song
      Zoltan Kodaly Chorus of Klara Leowey Secondary School
      Ilona Andor, cond.
      Choral Music IV -- Qualiton SLPX 11409

      Kodaly Girls Chorus of Budapest
      Ilona Andor, cond.
      Children's and Female Choruses -- Hungaroton SLPX 12492

Tell Me Where Is Fancy Bred
      Kodaly Girls Choir
      Ilona Andor, cond.
      Hungarian Songs -- Angel S-36334

Trieinia Hungarica (The Chamois; Fairey Veil; Opposite Is
            Badacsony Hill)
      Kodaly Choir of the Klara Leowey Secondary School
      Ilona Andor, cond.
      Choral Music II -- Hungaroton LPX 11315

Twelfth Night (1933)
      Zoltan Kodaly Girls Choir
      Ilona Andor, cond.
      Choral Music VII -- Hungaroton LPX 11612

Two Folksongs from Zobor
      Kodaly Choir of Debrecen
      Gyorgy Gulyas, cond.
      Qualiton LPX 1211 (1964)

Vejnemojnen makes Music (1944)
      Zoltan Kodaly Chorus of Klara Leowey Secondary School
      Ilona Andor, cond.
      Choral Music IV -- Qualiton SLPX 11409

      Kodaly Girls Chorus of Budapest
      Ilona Andor, cond.
      Children's and Female Choruses -- Hungaroton SLPX 12482

Vejnemojnen Plays (from Kalevala)
      Kodaly Choir of Debreceni
      Gyorgy Gulyas, cond.
      Qualiton LPX 1211 (1964)

Wainamoinen Makes Music
      Kodaly Girls Choir
      Ilona Andor, cond.
      Hungarian Songs -- Angel S-36334

Whitsuntide (1929)
      Columbus BoyChoir
      Donald Hanon, dir.
      The Columbus BoyChoir Performs Zoltan Kodaly --
            CBP Records CBP 675

      Kodaly Chorus of the Klara Leowey Secondary School
      Ilona Andor, cond.
      Choral Works II -- Hungaroton LPX 11315

      Kodaly Girls Choir
      Ilona Andor, cond.
      Hungarian Songs -- Angel S-36334

      Kodaly Girls Chorus of Budapest
      Ilona Andor, cond.
      Children's and Female Choruses -- Hungaroton SLPX 12492

   Wine Sweet Wine
      Lyons Township High School Treble Choir
      Lynne Bradley, dir.
      *Friends -- Delta DRS 81M 105

KOERPPEN, Alfred (1926-   )
      Joseph und seine Bruder
            Hanover Women's Choir
            Ludwig Rutt, cond.
            Camerata CMS 30.068 LPT

KOKKONEN, Joonas (1921-   )
      Paavo's Hymn (from The Last Temptations)
            The Tapiola Choir
            Erkki Pohjola, cond.
            Finlandia FA 327

KOREAN FOLK SONG
      Joyful Choon Hyang (arr. Hee Cho Kim)
            Ewha Women's University Chorus
            Mrs. Kyu-Soon Lee, cond.
            Choruses Of The World III

KOSTIAINEN, Jukka (1965-   )
     Concert
          The Tapiola Choir
          Erkki Pohjola, cond.
          Finlandia FA 327

     To Us A Festival Is Given
          The Tapiola Choir
          Erkki Pohjola, cond.
          Sounds of Finland -- Qualiton BIL LP-94

KOUNTZ, Richard (1896-1950)
     Prayer Of The Norweigan Child
          Alabama Music Educators All State
          Hugh Thomas, dir.
          *Alabama Music Educators Association 1978 --
               USC Sound Enterprise

KRAINTZ, Ken
     I'm Feelin' Right
          Lyons Township High School Treble Choir
          Lynne Bradley, dir.
          *Laudate Pueri Dominum a due Cori -- Delta DRS 78M 720A

KRENEK, Ernst (1900-   )
     Five Prayers over the Pater Noster (1. From being anxious
               or secure; 2. From needing danger to be good;
               3. Through thy submitting all; 4. Hear us, O hear
               us Lord!; 5. That learning, thine ambassador)
          The University of Southern California Dorians
          Michael Ingham, cond.
          *A Program of Music for Women's Voices from the 20th
               Century -- AEA 1094

          University Women's Glee Club, (University of Illinois)
          Russell Mathis, cond.
          *Custom Recording Studio -- CRS-7

     Two Choruses on Jacobean Poems
          The University of Southern California Dorians
          Michael Ingham, cond.
          *A Program of Music for Women's Voices from the 20th
               Century -- AEA 1094

KUBIK, Gail (1914-   )
     Scholastica: A Medieval Set (1972)
          Desto 7172

KUULA, Toivo (1883-1918)
     Evening (Illatunnelma)
          The Tapiola Choir
          Erkki Pohjola, dir.
          Sounds of Finland -- Qualiton BIS LP-94; Sounds of
               Tapiola -- Columbia 5.E-062-34670

LALLOUETTE, Jean Francois (1651-1728)
    O Mysterium ineffabile
        St. John's College
        George Guest
        In Quires and Places #12 -- Abbey LPB 730

LAMB, Thomas
    Abendstille
        Cincinnati BoysChoir
        William Dickinson, dir.
        *The Cincinnati All-City Boychoir

LANDINI, Francesco (1325-1397)
    Cosi pensoso cm' amor mi guida
        Vassar Madrigal Singers
        E. Harold Geer, cond.
        The Italian Madrigal: Ars Nova and the 16th c. --
            Allegro Records alg 3029

    De'l dimmi tu che se' cosi fregiato
        Vassar Madrigal Singers
        E. Harold Geer, cond.
        The Italian Madrigal: Ars Nova and the 16th c. --
            Allegro Records alg 3029

LANDOWSKI, Marcel (1915-   )
    Jesus, la es-tu?
        Maitrise de l'O.R.T.F.
        Jacques Jovineau, cond.
        Edici ED 41.010

    Quartre chants d'innocence
        Maitrise de l'O.R.T.F.
        Jacques Jovineau, cond.
        Edici ED 41.010

LANE, Philip (arr.)
    Lady Mary
        Cheltenham Ladies' College Choir
        Dorothy Dickinson, dir.
        Cantique -- Alpha APS 321

LANG, Istvan (1933-   )
    Fire (Tuz) (1974)
        Budapest Kodaly Zoltan Female Chorus
        Ilona Andor, dir.
        Contemporary Hungarian Female Choirs -- Hungaroton
            SLPX 11764

LANGLAIS, Jean (1907-   )
    Trois Oraisons: Salve Regina
        St. David's Cathedral Choir
        Nicolas Jackson, dir.
        Alpha APR 301

LASSUS, Orlando de (1583-1594)
    Adoramus Te Christe
        Lyons Township High School Treble Choir
        Lynne Bradley, dir.
        *(1975) Delta DRS 75-423

        The University Choir
        Richard Cox, dir.
        *Christmas Concert 1965 -- CSS 573-2103B

        York Minster Choir
        Francis Jackson, dir.
        Abbey LPB 695

    Magnum Opus Musicum (excerpts) (Contents: 1. Alleluia, laus
            et gloria; In pace in idipsum dormiam; Verbum
            caro a 3; Verbum caro a 4; 2. Agimus tibi gratias
            a 3 & a 4; 3. Adoramus Te I a 3; Adoramus Te II
            a 3; Doramus Te III a 5; 4. Beatus Vir; Beatus
            Homo; Occulus non vidit; 5. Cor Justus Expectatio
            justorum; Qui sequitur me; 6. Pro nuba lum)
        Girls Chorus of Gyor
        Miklos Szabo, dir.
        Qualiton LPX 11-441

    O Eyes Of My Beloved
        Clovis High School Treble Tones
        Wayne Anderson, dir.
        *Contest Selections 1981

LASZLO, Rossa
    Ma come bali bella bimba
        Hungarian Radio Children's Choir
        Botka & Csanyi, cond.
        Hungaroton SLPX 12163

LEGRAND, Michael
    Windmills Of Your Mind (arr. Philip Lane)
        Cheltenham Ladies' College Choir
        Dorothy Dickinson, dir.
        Cantique -- Alpha APS 321

LEIGH, Mitch (arr. James Aulenbach) (1928-   )
    The Impossible Dream
        The Aeolian Singers
        Claire Wall, dir.
        *The Impossible Dream Come True

LEIGH-COLEMAN
    El Sombero
        Salem College Choral Ensemble
        Paul W. Peterson, dir.
        *On The Campus and On The Road -- CMLP 1006

LEIGHTON, Kenneth (1929-   )
     God Is Ascended
          Choir of the Cathedral Church of All Saints, Wakefield
          Peter Gould, dir.
          In Quires and Places. . .#8 -- Abbey LPB 776

LEINBACH (ed.)
     Hosanna
          The Choral Ensemble of Salem College
          Paul Peterson, dir.
          *The Choral Ensemble of Salem College in Concert --
               XTV 62399

LEKBERG, Sven (1899-   )
     Let All The World In Every Corner Sing
          Lyons Township High School Treble Choir
          Lynne Bradley, dir.
          *(1977) -- Delta DRS 77M 621

          South Houston Girls Choir
          Sally Schott, dir.
          *Crest -- ACD-81-2B

LERNER-LOWE
     I Could Have Danced All Night
          The Choral Ensemble of Salem College
          Paul Peterson, dir.
          *The Choral Ensemble of Salem College in Concert --
               XTV 62399

LESUR, Daniel
     The Goat
          Hungarian Radio Children's Choir
          Botka & Csanyi, conds.
          Hungaroton SLPX 12163

LEUNER, Karl
     The Shepherd's Cradle Song (arr. Philip Lane)
          Cheltenham Ladies' College Choir
          Dorothy Dickinson, dir.
          Cantique -- Alpha APS 321

LEYDENS (arr.)
     We Beseech Thee
          Lyons Township High School Treble Choir
          Lynne Bradley, dir.
          *Patterns in Music -- Delta DRS 74-139A

LILJESTRAND, Paul
     Three Canticles for Treble Voices (1973) (Contents: Tune
          Me, O Lord; The Masters Touch; The Mirror)
          Bethel College Women's Choir
          Mary Fall, cond.
          *(1979)

LIONCOURT, Guy (1885-1961)
    Quid retribuam Domino
        Chichester Cathedral Choir
        Alan Thurlow, cond.
        O Praise God In His Holiness -- Abbey APS 317

LISZT, Franz (1811-1886)
    An den Wassern zu Babylon (Psalm 137)
        Gyor Female Choir
        Miklos Szabo, dir.
        Qualiton SLPX 11381

    Hymn de l'Enfant a Son Reveil (1877)
        Female Choir of Gyor
        Hungaroton LPX 11381

    O heilige Nacht, G 49
        Gyor Female Choir
        Miklos Szabo, dir.
        Liszt Choral Works -- Qualiton SLPX 11381

    O Salutaris, G 43
        Gyor Female Choir
        Miklos Szabo, dir.
        Liszt Choral Works -- Qualiton SLPX 11381

    Tantum Ergo, G 42
        Gyor Female Choir
        Miklos Szabo, dir.
        Liszt Choral Works -- Qualiton SLPX 11381

LITAIZE, Gaston (1909-   )
    It Is Christmas
        Boys of Reims Cathedral Choir
        Arsene Mazerelle, dir.
        Christmas in the Great Cathedral of Reims -- MHS 818

LLOYD, Richard
    Prayer
        Chapel Choir of the Blue Coat School, Birmingham
        Hugh Shelton, dir.
        Abbey LPB 766

LOESSER, Frank (1910-1969)
    Standing On The Corner (Stickles)
        Salem College Choral Ensemble
        Paul W. Peterson, dir.
        *On The Campus and On The Road -- CMLP 1006

LONDON, Edwin (1929-   )
    Better Is
        Smith College Chamber Singers
        Iva Dee Hiatt, dir.
        Ubres Recordings CS 302

    Dream Thing in Biblical Episodes
        Smith College Chamber Singers
        Iva Dee Hiatt, dir.
        Ubres Recordings CS 302

LOTTI, Antonio (1667-1740)
    Ecce Panis Angelorum
        Hungarian Radio Children's Choir
        Botka & Csanyi, conds.
        Hungaroton SLPX 12163

    Vere Languores Nostros (arr. Hunter)
        Miami Girls Chorus
        Lynne Huff, cond.
        *HIS Recording

        Mississippi University for Women Chapel Choir
        Marilyn Swingle, dir.
        *

LUMSFORD, David
    Responses and Preces
        The Choristers of Chester Cathedral
        Roger Fisher, dir.
        The Choristers of Chester Cathedral At Evensong --
            Vista VAS 2001

MAHLER, Gustav (1860-1911)
    Symphony #3
        Ambrosian Singers and Wandsworth School Boys Choir
        London Symphony/Horenstein
        Nonesuch 73023

        Ambrosian Chorus and Wandsworth School Boys Choir
        London Symphony/Solti
        Lonson 2223

        Women of Chicago Symphony Chorus and Glen Ellyn
            Children's Choir
        Chicago Symphony
        RCA ARL 2-1757 (Levine); London 72014 (Solti)

Symphony #3 (continued)
>Women of London Symphony Orchestra Chorus and Southend
>>Boys Chorus
>London Symphony/Tennstedt
>Angel DS 3902

>Members of Los Angeles Master Chorale and California
>>Boys Chorus
>Los Angeles Philharmonic/Mehta
>London CSA 2249

>Women of Netherlands Radio Chorus and Boys Chorus of
>>St. Willibrod's Church
>Concertgebouw/Haitink
>Philips PHS 2-996

>Schola Cantorum & Boys
>New York Philharmonic/Bernstein
>Columbia M2S 675

>Utah Symphony Chorus
>Utah Symphony/Abravanel
>Vanguard C-10072/3

MAINVILLE, Denise
>Lord Make Me An Instrument Of Thy Peace
>>Bethel College Women's Choir
>>Oliver Mogck, dir.
>>*(1972)

MALLORD and MORROW
>Little Dove
>>Boys' Choir of St. Mary's Hall, Stonyhurst
>>Harry Duckworth, dir.
>>Pueri Sanctae Mariae -- Alpha APS 322

>Peace Song, The
>>Boys' Choir of St. Mary's Hall, Stonyhurst
>>Harry Duckworth, dir.
>>Pueri Sanctae Mariae -- Alpha APS 322

MALOTTE, Albert Hay (1895-   )
>The Lord Is My Shepherd (arr. Downing)
>>Moody Women's Glee Club
>>Robert Carbaugh, dir.
>>*Moody IV -- Moody Bible Institute

MARCELLO, Bendetto (1686-1739)
>Give Ear Unto Me (ed. Philip Ledger)
>>Cheltenham Ladies' College Choir
>>Dorothy Dickinson, dir.
>>Cantique -- Alpha APS 321

MARTIN, Frank (1890-1974)
    Ode (pour 2 voix de femme et violoncello)
        Communaute de travail pour la diffusion de la musique
            suisse -- CTS 47

MARTINI, Giovanni Baptista (1706-1784)
    On Monte Oliveti
        The Tapiola Choir
        Erkki Pohjola, dir.
        Sounds of Tapiola -- Columbia 5.E.062-34670

MASCAGNI, Pietro (1863-1945)
    Anthem For Spring
        New Mexico All State Girls Choir
        John D. Raymond, dir.
        *New Mexico Music Educators Association 1968 --
            Century Stereo 29256

MATHIAS, William (1934-   )
    A Carol Sequence, Op. 89
        Cheltenham Ladies' College Choir
        Dorothy Dickinson, dir.
        Alpha ACA 519

MAYFIELD, Larry
    Rejoice The Lord Is King
        Moody Women's Glee Club
        Robert Carbaugh, dir.
        *Moody IV -- Moody Bible Institute

    Songs Of The People
        Moody Women's Glee Club
        Robert Carbaugh, dir.
        *Moody IV -- Moody Bible Institute

MAYSHUET (Matheus de Sancto Johanne) (1365-1389)
    Motet: Arae post Libamina/Nunc Surgent
        The Columbia University Collegium Musicum
        Richard Taruslein, dir.
        Music of the Henrys of England -- Collegium Records

McCRAY, James
    Rise Up My Love
        Wells College Choir
        Crawford R. Thoburn, dir.
        *(1879-1980)

MELLANAS, Arne (1933-   )
    Aglepta
        The Tapiola Choir
        Erkki Pohjola, dir.
        Sounds of Tapiola -- Columbia 5.E.062-34670; Deutsche
            Gramophon 2530.812

MENDELSSOHN, Felix (1809-1847)
    Caro cibus
        London Oratory Junior Choir
        John Hoban, dir.
        Abbey MVP 782

    Good and Patient Shepherd, A
        (SEE: Surrexit Christus)

    Happy and Blest Are They (St. Paul)
        Mississippi University for Women Chapel Choir
        Marilyn Swingle, dir.
        *

    He Watching Over Israel
        The Sullins Choir
        Leon B. Fleming, Jr., dir.
        Recorded Publications E4QL2071 (1953-1954)

    Incidental Music to "A Midsummer Night's Dream" Op. 21 & 61
        Women's Voices of the Mendelssohn Choir of Philadelphia
        Robert Page, dir.
        RCA ARL 1-2084 (1977)

    Laudate pueri Dominum, Op. 39, #2
        Choir of St. Michael's College, Tenbury
        Roger Judd, dir.
        The Choir of St. Michael's College, Tenbury -- Abbey
            APR 303

        Mississippi University for Women Chapel Choir
        Marilyn Swingle, dir.
        *

        University Choir
        Richard Cox, dir.
        *Christmas Concert 1964 -- CSS 423-1598A; *Christmas
            Concert 1967 -- Robbins 1911-A

        Women of Stuttgart Chamber Choir
        Frieder Bernius, dir.
        Spectrum SR-103 (1979)

    Lift Thine Eyes (Elijah)
        The Chapel Singers
        Paul Peterson, dir.
        *The Choral Ensemble of Salem College in Concert --
            XTV 62399

        Women of Mormon Tabernacle Choir
        Richard Condie, dir.
        Lift Thine Eyes -- Columbia P 14244

Lift Thine Eyes (continued)
        Women of Mormon Tabernacle Choir
        J. Spender Cornwall, dir.
        Columbia ML 2077 (1949)

        Obernkirchen Children's Choir
        Edith Moeller
        Songs and a Wonderful Story -- Angel 35684

        St. Paul's Cathedral Boys Choir
        Rejoice -- K-Tel NE 1064

        Choristers of Worcester Cathedral
        Abbey LPB 764

Surrexit Christus, Op. 39, #3
        Mississippi University for Women Chapel Choir
        Marilyn Swingle, dir.
        *

        Wheaton College Women's Chorale
        Mary Hopper, cond.
        *Let All The World In Every Corner Sing -- WETN
            820-501

Three motets, Op. 39 (1. Veni Domine; 2. Laudate pueri;
            3. Surrexit)
        Kodaly Girls Choir
        Ilona Andor, cond.
        Hungaroton SLPX 11-862

Veni Dominum, Op. 39, #1
        The London Oratory Junior Choir
        John Hoban, dir.
        Laetare Jerusalem -- Abbey MVP 782

        The University Choir
        Richard Cox, dir.
        *Christmas Concert 1964 -- CSS 423 1598A

Ye Sons of Israel (SEE: Laudate Pueri)

MENNIN, Peter (1923-1983)
    Bought Locks
        Agnes Scott College Glee Club
        Richard Hensel, dir.
        *Agnes Scott College Glee Club Spring Concert 1964

MERCURE, Georges (1905-   )
    Adaptations gregoriennes
        Choeur des Moniales benedictine du Precieux-Sang
        Monials benedictine du Precieus-Sang BML 47

    Last Words of Christ on the Cross
        Choeur des Monials Benedictius du Precieus-Sang
        M. Laurier, cond.
        Polyphonie gregorienne a quatre voix egales -- Monials
            Benedictines du Precieux-Sang BML 1-2

    Messe solennelle du jour de Paques
        Chanteus de Saint-Dominique
        Roland Seguin, cond.
        Moniales benedictines du Precieus-Sang BML 10

    Ordinare de messe et cantique
        Choir of Moniales benedictines du Precieux-Sang
        Liturgie des jeunes -- BML 11

    Prions avec le rois David
        Choir of Moniales benedictines du Precieux-Sang
        Liturgie des Jeunes -- BML 11

MERIKANTO, Oskar (1868-1924)
    Do You Remember Still That Hymn
        The Tapiola Choir
        Erkki Pohjola, cond.
        Finlandia FA 327

MESSIAEN, Oliver (1908-   )
    Trois petites liturgies de la Presence Divine
        Women's Chorus of Choral Art Society
        New York Philharmonic/Bernstein
        Columbia MS 6582 (1964); Columbia ML 5982 (1964)

        Choeurs de la Maitrese
        Marcel Couraud, cond.
        Music Guild MG-142; MS-142 (1966); Also Erato
            STU 70200 (197?)

        Female Chorus of the O.R.T.F.
        Marcel Couraud, cond.
        MHS 1820 (1974)

        Mergaieiu Choras Liepaites
        Saulis Sondeckis, cond.
        Melodia (1978)

MIKOLAJ of Radom (c. 1430)
    Patrem Omnipotentem
        Women of Pomeranian Philharmonia of Bydgoszcz
        Stanislaw Galonski
        Polish Medieval Music -- MHS OR 341

MILHAUD, Darius (1892-   )
    Deux Elegies Romaines De Goethe
        The University of Southern California Dorians
        Michael Ingham, cond.
        *A Program of Music for Women's Voices from the 20th
            Century -- AEA 1094

MILLER, Carl
    El Zapatero (from Canciones de los Ninos)
        Miami Girls Chorus
        Lynne Huff, cond.
        *HIS Recording

MILLS, F.
    Little Music Box Dancer
        The Aeolian Singers
        Claire Wall, dir.
        *The Impossible Dream Come True

MOE, Daniel (1926-   )
    O Holy Spirit Enter In
        Bethel College Women's Choir
        Oliver Mogck, dir.
        *(Gold Cover)

MOELLER, F. W.
    Snow White
        Obernkirchen Children's Choir
        Edith Moeller, cond.
        Angel 35684

MOGCK, Oliver (arr.)
    Angels In Shining Order Stand (Sacred Harp)
        Bethel College Women's Choir
        Oliver Mogck, dir.
        *(Gold Cover)

MONTEVERDI, Claudio (1567-1643)
    Sacrae Cantiuncula (Contents: Lapidabant Stephanum; Veni in
            hortum meum; Ego sum Pastor bonus; Surge propera;
            Ubi duo; Quam pulchra es; Ave Maria; Domine
            pater; Tu es pastor 1 & 2; O magnum pietatis; Eli
            Clamans; O Crux benedicta; Hodie Christus natus
            est; O domine Jesu 1 & 2; Pater venit hora; In
            tua patientia; Angelus ad pastores ait; Salve
            crux poetiosa; Quia vidisti me; Lauda Sion
            Salvatorem; O Bone Jesu; Surgens Jesus; Qui vult
            venire; Iusti tulerunt spolia)
        Gyor Girls Choir
        Miklos Szabo, dir.
        Hungaroton SLPX 11937

Sonata a 8 sopra "Sancta Maria ora pro nobis"
    Sopranos of St. Hedwig's Cathedral
    Carl Gorvin, cond.
    Archiv ARC 3005 (1955)

MORALES, Cristobal de (1500-1553)
  O magnum Mysterium
    University Treble Choir (Illinois State University)
    Donald Armstrong, dir.
    *

    University of Virginia Women's Chorus
    Katherine Mitchell, dir.
    *Candlelight Christmas -- 8393

MORAVIAN
  An Evening Prayer
    The Choral Ensemble of Salem College
    Paul Peterson, dir.
    The Choral Ensemble of Salem College in Concert --
      XTV 62399

MORLEY, Thomas (1557-1602)
  Fire, Fire My Heart
    Agnes Scott College Glee Club
    Richard Hensel, dir.
    *Agnes Scott College Spring Concert 1964

  My Bonnie Lass (arr. K. K. Davis)
    The Choral Ensemble of Salem College
    Paul Peterson, dir.
    *The Choral Ensemble Of Salem College in Concert --
      XTV 62399

  Now Is the Month Of Maying
    Choral Ensemble of Salem College
    Paul Peterson, dir.
    *The Choral Ensemble of Salem College in Concert --
      XTV 62399

    (in Hungarian)
    Hungarian Radio Children's Chorus
    Botka & Csanyi, conds.
    Hungaroton SLPX 12163

    Salem Academy Glee Club
    Jean Burroughs, dir.
    *(1978-79) -- Z530071

Sing We And Chant It
        Choral Ensemble of Salem College
        Paul Peterson, dir.
        *The Choral Ensemble of Salem College in Concert --
            XTV 62399

        Philomela
        Susan Ames-Zierman, dir.
        Many Butterflies -- RBR 001

MORSE, Judith
    Alma Mater
        Wheelock College Glee Club
        Leo Collins, dir.
        *Vogts Quality Recording

MOZART, Wolfgang A. (1856-1791)
    Adoramus Te
        Mississippi University for Women Chapel Choir
        Marilyn Swingle, dir.
        *

    Agnus Dei
        The Salem Academy Glee Club
        Jean Burroughs, dir.
        *(1978-79) -- Z 530071

    Canons
        (Contents: Alleluia, K.553; Ave Maria, K.554; Bona
            Nox!, K.561; Caro bell' idol mio, K. 562;
            Difficile lectu mihi mars, K.559; Essen, Trinken,
            K.234(382e); Gehn wir im Prater, K.558;
            Grechtelt's enk, K.556; Kyrie, K.89 (73k);
            Lacrimoso son' io K.555; Lasst froh uns sein,
            K.231 (382c); Lieber Freistadtler, lieber
            Gaulimauli K.232(509a); Nascoso e il mio sol,
            K.557; Nichts labt mich mehr als Wein, K.233
            (382d); O du eselhfter Peierl, K.560a; Selig,
            Selig K.230 (382b); Sie ist dahin, K.229 (382a)
        Gyor Girls Choir
        Miklos Szabo, cond.
        Hungaroton SLPD 12373

    Kanon
        Cincinnati BoysChoir
        William Dickinson, dir.
        *Cincinnati BoysChoir 1980-81

    Komm, lieber Mai
        Vienna Choir Boys
        Romantic Vienna -- Everest SDBR 3240

Kyrie for Five Sopranos, K. 73
        Choirs of St. Bartholomews Church and Hospital
        Abbey LPB 773

        Gyor Girls Choir
        Miklos Szabo, dir.
        Hungaroton SLPD 12373

    Laudate Dominum
        Mississippi University for Women Chapel Choir
        Marilyn Swingle, dir.
        *

        The Sullins Choir
        Leon B. Fleming, Jr., dir.
        Recorded Publications E4QL2071 (1953-1954)

    We Worship Thee
        Bethel College Women's Choir
        Mary Fall, cond.
        *(1976)

MYSLIVECEK, Joseph (1737-1781)
    Notturnos for 2 female voices & Orchestra
        Musici Pragenes
        Parthias and Notturnos -- Supraphon SUA ST 59665

NAKADA, Yoshinao
    A behavazott varosban
        Hungarian Radio Children's Choir
        Botka & Csanyi, conds.
        Hungaroton SLPX 12163

NANINO, Giovanni (1560-1623)
    Laetamini Domino
        Choir of Mary Baldwin College
        George Page, dir.
        *Richmond Sound Stage 10725

NARES, James (1715-1783)
    The Souls Of The Righteous
        St. John's College
        George Guest, cond.
        English Cathedral Music: 1770-1860 -- Argo ZRG 5406

    The Voice Of Joy
        Choristers of Chester Cathedral
        Roger Fisher, dir.
        The Choristers of Chester Cathedral At Evensong --
            Vista VAS 2001

NATAL BRASILEIRO
     (collection of carols)
          Canarinhos de Petropolis
          Alceo Bocchino, cond.
          Radio Ministerio de Educacao e Cultura -- PRA 2-1003
               (1966)

NEHLYBEL, Vaclav (1919-   )
     Peter Gray
          Washington High School Choir
          Karen Bushman-Villilo, dir.
          *Washington High School Choir Spring Concert - 1976

NELSON, Ron (1929-   )
     He Came Here For Me
          Salem College Choral Ensemble
          Paul W. Peterson, dir.
          *On The Campus and On The Road -- CMLP 1006

     He's Gone Away (from Three Mountain Ballads)
          Lyons Township High School Treble Choir
          Lynne Bradley, dir.
          *(1975) -- Delta DRS 75 423

NEUSS, Heinrich (1654-1716)
     Die Schonste von allen (1935)
          Choir of the State High School for Music
          MHS 1492

NEWBURY, Kent (1925-   )
     Arise, My Love
          Lyons Township High School Treble Choir
          Lynne Bradley, dir.
          *Laudate Pueri Dominum a due Cori -- Delta DRS 78M
               720A

     O Come Let Us Sing Unto The Lord
          Bethel College Women's Choir
          Oliver Mogck, dir.
          *(1972)

     Psalm 150
          Lyons Township High School Treble Choir
          Lynne Bradley, dir.
          *(1979) -- Delta DRS 79M 614

     Wisdom and Understanding
          Lyons Township High School Treble Choir
          Lynne Bradley, dir.
          *Patterns in Music -- Delta DRS 72-139A

NILES, John Jacob (1892-1980)
    I Wonder as I Wander
        Choir of S. Mary & S. Anne
        Llywela Harris, dir.
        Ave Maria: A Celebration of Carols -- Alpha APS 315

NONO, Luigi (1924-   )
    Canciones a Guioma
        Womens Choir & Berlin Radio Symphony
        Bruno Maderna, cond.
        Primadonnen der Moderne -- Hor zu Black Label SHZW
            800 BL

    Ha Venido -- canciones para Silva (1960)
        Sopranchor der Stuttgart Schola Cantorum
        Clytus Gottwald, dir.
        Wergo WER 60-038

    Ricorda cosa ti hanno fatto in Auschwitz (1965)
        Kinderchor des Piccolo Teatro, Mailand
        Wergo WER 60-038

NOVA SCOTIA FOLK SONG
    The Old Men
        The Aeolian Singers
        Claire Wall, dir.
        *The Impossible Dream Come True

NYSTEDT, Knut (1915-   )
    Hosanna
        Lyons Township High School Treble Choir
        Lynne Bradley, dir.
        *Bursting Out -- Delta DRS 82M 116

    Seek Ye The Lord
        Radcliffe Choral Society
        Beverly Taylor, cond.
        AFKA Records SK 4674

OGURA, Akira (arr.)
    Hotaru Koi (nursery song from Akita province, Japan)
        The Tapiola Choir
        Erkki Pohjola, dir.
        Sounds of Finland -- Qualiton BIS LP 94

ORFF, Carl (1895-   )
    Carol settings (Contents: The Crib; Ding Dong Merrily On
            High; Good King Wenceslas; Patapan; Silent Night;
            The Sussex Carol
        Choir of Girls from Ashford
        Victrola VICS 1376

Music For Children (das Schulwerk)
        Choruses of the Children's Opera Group and Choruses
            of the Bancroft School For Boys
        Angel 3582

ORTOLANI and OLIVIERO
    More
        Salem College Choral Ensemble
        Paul W. Paterson, dir.
        *On The Campus and On The Road -- CMLP 1006

OWEN-PROTHEROE-WATSON
    Laudamus
        Bethel College Women's Choir
        Mary Fall, cond.
        *(1976)

OXLEY, Harrison
    Mater Ora Filium
        Southend Boys Choir
        Michael Crabb, dir.
        Christmas Music -- Vista VPS 1068

PACIS, Fredrik (1809-1891)
    Our Country
        The Tapiola Choir
        Erkki Pohjola, dir.
        Sounds of Finland -- Qualiton BIS LP 94

    Song of Suomi
        The Tapiola Choir
        Erkki Pohjola, dir.
        Sounds of Finland -- Qualiton BIS LP 94

PADEREWSKI, Ignacy Jan (1860-1941)
    Menuet a l'Antique
        Peninsula Women's Chorus
        Patricia Hennings, dir.
        *Song of Survival

PAGOT, Jean
    It's Christmas Day
        Reims Cathedral Choir
        Arsene Mazerelle, dir.
        Christmas in the Great Cathedral of Reims -- MHS 818

PALESTRINA, G. P. (1525-1594)
    Adoramus Te, Christe
        Gyor Girls Choir
        Miklos Szabo, dir.
        Hungaroton SLPX 11328

        Period Choral Society
        Robert Strassburg, cond.
        A Concert of A Capella Music for Treble Voices --
            Period Records SPL 513

    Alma Redemptoris Mater
        Gyor Girls Choir
        Miklos Szabo, dir.
        Hungaroton SLPX 11328

    Ave Maria
        Gyor Girls Choir
        Miklos Szabo, dir.
        Hungaroton SLPX 11328

    Ave Regina Caelorum
        Gyor Girls Choir
        Miklos Szabo, dir.
        Hungaroton SLPX 11328

        University Treble Choir (Illinois State University)
        Donald Armstrong, dir.
        *A Choral Christmas

    Ahi che quest' occhi miei
        Vassar Madrigal Singers
        E. Harold Geer, cond.
        The Italian Madrigal: Ars Nova and the 16th c. --
            Allegro Records alg 3029

    Benedictus (from Missa Descendit Angelus Domini)
        Period Choral Society
        Robert Strassburg, cond.
        A Concert of A Capella Music for Treble Voices --
            Period Records SPL 513

    Confitemini Domino
        Gyor Girls Choir
        Miklos Szabo, dir.
        Hungaroton SLPX 11328

        Period Choral Society
        Robert Strassburg, cond.
        A Concert of A Capella Music for Treble Voices --
            Period Records SPL 513

Crucifixus (from Missa O Rex Gloriae)
    Mississippi University for Women Chapel Choir
    Marilyn Swingle, dir.
    *

    Period Choral Society
    Robert Strassburg, cond.
    A Concert of A Capella Music for Treble Voices --
        Period Records SPL 513

Da cosi dotta man sei stato fatto
    Vassar Madrigal Singers
    E. Harold Geer, cond.
    The Italian Madrigal: Ars Nova and the 16th c. --
        Allegro Records alg 3029

Gloriosi principes terrae
    Gyor Girls Choir
    Miklos Szabo, dir.
    Hungaroton SLPX 11328

Haec Dies
    Gyor Girls Choir
    Miklos Szabo, dir.
    Hungaroton SLPX 11328

Hodie Christus Natus Est
    Radcliffe Choral Society
    Nadia Boulanger, cond.
    Greenough #264b (Library of Congress)

    Period Choral Society
    Robert Strassburg, cond.
    A Concert of A Capella Music for Treble Voices --
        Period Records SPL 513

    The University Choir
    Richard Cox, dir.
    *Christmas Concert 1965 -- CSS 573-2103B

Jesus Rex admirabilis
    Hungarian Radio Children's Choir
    Botka & Csanyi, conds.
    Hungaroton SLPX 12163

    Period Choral Society
    Robert Strassburg, cond.
    A Concert of A Capella Music for Treble Voices --
        Period Records SPL 513

Magnificat (IV Toni cum quatuor vocibus paribus)
    Gyor Girls Choir
    Miklos Szabo, dir.
    Hungaroton SLPX 11937

Magnificat in 4th mode (for women's voices & plainchant)
    Dessoff Choirs
    P. Boepple, cond.
    Sacred Music -- Counterpoint 602

    Period Choral Society
    Robert Strassburg, cond.
    A Concert of A Capella Music for Treble Voices --
        Period Records SPL 513

Missa 'Sine Nomine' (Missa 'Montovana')
    Gyor Girls Choir
    Miklos Szabo, dir.
    Hungaroton SLPX 11328

O Bone Jesu
    Mississippi University for Women Chapel Choir
    Marilyn Swingle, dir.
    *

Pleni Sunt Coeli (Missa Sacerdotes Domini)
    Period Choral Society
    Robert Strassburg, cond.
    A Concert of A Capella Music for Treble Voices --
        Period Records SPL 513

Pueri Hebraeorum
    Gyor Girls Choir
    Miklos Szabo, dir.
    Hungaroton SLPX 11328

Salve Regina
    Gyor Girls Choir
    Miklos Szabo, dir.
    Hungaroton SLPX 11328

    Period Choral Society
    Robert Strassburg, cond.
    A Concert of A Capella Music for Treble Voices --
        Period Records SPL 513

Sub Tuum Praesidium
    Gyor Girls Choir
    Miklos Szabo, dir.
    Hungaroton SLPX 11328

Surrexit pastor bonus
    Gyor Girls Choir
    Miklos Szabo, dir.
    Hungaroton SLPX 11328

Tua Jesu Dilectio
        Period Choral Society
        Robert Strassburg, cond.
        A Concert of A Capella Music for Treble Voices --
            Period Records SPL 513

    We Adore Thee (arr. H. Morgan)
        Bethel College Women's Choir
        Mary Fall, cond.
        *(1979)

PANULA, Jorma (1930-   )
    Are You Sleeping
        The Tapiola Choir
        Erkki Pohjola, dir.
        Deutsche Graophon 2530.812

    Evening Song
        The Tapiola Choir
        Erkki Pohjola, dir.
        Sounds of Finland -- Qualiton BIS LP 94

PAPP, Akos (arr.)
    Burro Matti (Lappish Jojk)
        The Tapiola Choir
        Erkki Pohjola, dir.
        Sounds of Finland -- Qualiton BIS LP 94

    Tuku Tuku Lampaitani (A Call For Sheep)
        The Tapiola Choir
        Erkki Pohjola, dir.
        Sounds of Tapiola -- Columbia 5.3-062-34670

PEETERS, Flor (1903-   )
    Sing To God With Gladness (Ps.99)
        Bethel College Women's Choir
        Oliver Mogck, dir.
        *(Gold Cover)

        Mississippi University for Women Chapel Choir
        Marilyn Swingle, dir.
        *

PENHORWOOD, Edwin
    Mother Goose On The Loose
        University Of Georgia Women's Glee Club
        Ann Jones, cond.
        *Crest S-ACDA-80-3A

PENNINGER, David (1929-   )
    Little Things That Creep and Crawl and Sometimes Fly (Mice;
            The Puzzled Centipede; A Fish Wish; White
            Butterflies)
        Columbia College Choir
        Gutherie Darr, dir.
        *Crest ACD-81-3a

PERGOLESI, Giovanni Battista (1710-1736)
    Amen (final chorus of Stabat Mater)
        The Tapiola Choir
        Erkki Pohjola, cond.
        Deutsche Gramophon 2530.812

    Fac Ut Ardeat Cor Meum (from Stabat Mater)
        Salem Academy Glee Club
        Jean Burroughs, dir.
        *(1980-81) -- Recorded Publications Z-577041

    Glory To God In The Highest
        Salem Academy Glee Club
        Jean Burroughs, dir.
        *(1980-81) -- Recorded Publications Z 577041

    Psalm 51 (arr. J.S. Bach)
        Womens Voices of Bach Choir of Mainz
        Diethard Hellmann, cond.
        MHS-1677 (1974)

    Stabat Mater
        (opening chorus)
        Choir of S. Mary & S. Anne
        Llywela Harris, dir.
        Ave Maria: A Celebration of Carols -- Alpha APS 315

        Czech Philharmonic Chorus
        Prague Chamber Orchestra/Bruni
        Supraphon 1 12.0620

        Women of Hungarian Radio & TV Chorus and Franz Liszt
            Chamber Orchestra/Gardelli
        Supraphon SLPX 12201

        Madrigal Chorus of Cologne and Cologne Bach Orchestra
        Mace M9014

        (selections)
        New England Preparatory School Music Festival Chorus
        Lorna Coole deVaron, cond.
        TransRadio TR-988 MG7-201,337

Stabat Mater (continued)
       Nottingham Oriana Choir
       Roy Henderson, dir.
       Decca LXT 6907 (1978)

       Women's voices of RIAS Chamber Chorus
       Berlin Radio Orchestra/Maazel
       Philips 6540-045 or 6570-123

       St. John's College, Cambridge
       George Guest, cond.
       Argo ZRG 913

       Women's chorus of Teatro Communale with Chamber
             Orchestra of Teatro Communale
       MHS MH504 (Re-issue of Epic LC 3460)

       Vienna Academy Chamber Choir
       Vanguard SRV 195; Vanguard BG 549

   Quando Corpus Morietur and Amen (Stabat Mater)
       Mississippi University for Women Chapel Choir
       Marilyn Swingle, dir.
       *

PERSICHETTI, Vincent (1915-   )
   glad and very (5 e.e. cummings choruses: 1. little man; i
             am so glad and very; 3. maybe god; 4. jake hates
             all the girls; 5. a politician)
       University Womens Chorus
       William McIver, cond.
       *Crest S-ACDA-80-5B

   Hist Whist
       Agnes Scott College Glee Club
       Richard Hensel, dir.
       *Agnes Scott College Glee Club Spring Concert

       Shenandoah Chorus
       Robert McSpadden, cond.
       *Festival of Music -- V25575-3

   Love
       Mendelssohn Club of Philadelphia
       Tamara Brooks, cond.
       New World Records -- NW-316

   Spring Cantata
       Wheelock College Glee Club
       Leo Collins, dir.
       *Vogts Quality Recording

This Is A Garden
>The University Of North Carolina Choir
>Richard Cox, dir.
>*Twentieth Century Compositions for Treble Voices --
>>CSS 554

Winter Cantata, Op. 97
>Mendelssohn Club of Philadelphia
>Tamara Brooks, cond.
>New World Records -- NW-316

PETER, Johann Frederick (1746-1813)
>I Will Be As The Morning Dew
>>Salem College Choral Ensemble
>>Paul W. Peterson, dir.
>>*On The Campus and On The Road -- CMLP 1006

PETROVICS, Emil (1930-   )
>Cantata #4 - We All Depart (1980)
>>Ladies of the Hungarian Radio and TV Chorus
>>Ferenec Sapzon, dir.
>>Hungaroton SLPX 12320

The Music Of The Seasons (1967) (Contents: 1. Winter
>Advice for Myself; 2. March; 3. Raindrops;
>4. Deadly Apollo; 5. Night Music; 6. Late Autumn
>Little Song; 7. Epilogue)
>Budapest Kodaly Zoltan Female Choir
>Ilona Andor, cond.
>Contemporary Hungarian Female Choirs -- Hungaroton
>>SLPX 11764

PFAUTSCH, Lloyd (1921-   )
>A Hymn Of Him Of True Love
>>Lyons Township High School Treble Choir
>>Lynne Bradley, dir.
>>*(1975) -- Delta DRS 75-423

Annunciation
>Lyons Township High School Treble Choir
>Lynne Bradley, dir.
>*(1977) -- Delta DRS 77M 621

Five Narrative Carols
>The University Of North Carolina - Greensboro Choir
>Richard Cox, dir.
>*Christmas Concert 1969 -- CCSS 1082

Laughing Song
>Lyons Township High School Treble Choir
>Lynne Bradley, dir.
>*(1976)

Spring
    East Carolina University Women's Glee Club
    Rhonda Fleming, dir.
    *HIS Recording

PHILLIPS
  Dream Agnus
    The Aeolian Singers
    Claire Wall, dir.
    *The Impossible Dream Comes True

PIERPOINT, J.
  Jingle Bells
    The Salem Academy Glee Club
    Jean Burroughs, dir.
    *(1978-1979) -- Z 530071

PINKHAM, Daniel (1923-   )
  Angelus Pastorus Est
    Lyons Township High School Treble Choir
    Lynne Bradley, dir.
    *(1976)

  Ave Maria
    The Glen Ellyn Children's Chorus
    Doreen Rao, cond.
    *Delta/Stereo DRS 76M 536

  Company At The Creche
    The Dale Warland Singers
    Dale Warland, cond.
    Sing Noel - Christmas Music of Daniel Pinkham --
        Augsburg 23-1917

  Five Canzonets
    Wells College Choir
    Crawford R. Thoburn, dir.
    *(1979-80)

  Hinder Not Music (from Five Motets)
    The Glen Ellyn Children's Chorus
    Doreen Rao, cond.
    *Delta/Stereo DRS 76M 536

  Love's Yoke
    Lyons Township High School Treble Choir
    Lynne Bradley, dir.
    *Crest NC-ACDA-80-6A

  Magnificat
    The Dale Warland Singers
    Dale Warland, cond.
    Sing Noel - Christmas Music of Daniel Pinkham --
        Augsburg 23-1917

Spring (from Five Canzonets)
        The Glen Ellyn Children's Chorus
        Doreen Rao, cond.
        *Delta/Stereo DRS 76M 536

Three Lenten Poems of Richard Crashaw
        Wheelock College Glee Club
        Leo Collins, cond.
        *Vogts Quality Recording

PITONI, Giuseppe Ottovio (1657-1743)
    Cantate Domino
        (sung in Hungarian)
        Hungarian Radio Children's Chorus
        Botka & Czanyi, conds.
        Hungaroton SLPX 12163

PLAINSONG (12th c.)
    Ave Maria (Salutation Carol) (arr. Imogen Holst)
        Choir of S. Mary & S. Anne
        Llywela Harris, dir.
        Ave Maria: A Celebration of Carols -- Alpha APS 315

    O Come Emmanuel
        Wells College Glee Club
        Crawford R. Thoburn, cond.
        *(1979-80)

PORPORA, Nicola (1686-1768)
    Magnificat (ed. Hunter)
        St. Joseph's Academy
        Sister Joan M. Whittenmore, cond.
        *Christmas Record (1978)

        Smith College Glee Club
        Iva Dee Hiatt, dir.
        College Choirs at Christmas -- Classics Record
            Library #10-5573, side 5

PORTER, Cole (1892-1964)
    Night and Day
        The Salem Academy Glee Club
        Jean Burroughs, dir.
        *(1978-79) -- Recorded Publications Z 530071

POSTON, E. (1905-   )
    Jesus Christ The Apple Tree
        Choir of the School of St. Mary & St. Anne
        Llywela Harris, dir.
        Day By Day -- Argo ZRG 785

POULENC, Francis (1899-1963)
    Ave Maria
        Girls Glee of Terry Parker High School
        H. Hampton Kicklighter, dir.
        *Custom Directors Recording -- DR 8379/zZ4RS 5194

    Litanies a la Vierge Noire
        Women of Le Groupe Vocale de France
        John Alldis, cond.
        EMI C-69-73030

        Jean de Ockeghem vocal ensemble
        Claude Panterne, cond.
        ERATO MHS 1035 (1970)

        Maitrise d'enfants
        Jacques Jouineau
        Pathe DTX 247

        The Peloquin Chorale
        C. Alexander Peloquin, cond.
        Gregorian Institute 205

        Radcliffe Choral Society
        Nadia Boulanger, cond.
        Greenough #267A, 266B, 267B (Library of Congress)

        St. John's College, Cambridge
        George Guest, cond.
        O Sacrum Convivium -- Argo ZRG 662

        Worcester Cathedral Choir
        Donald Hunt, dir.
        French Choral Music -- Abbey LPB 780

    Petites Voix (only: La Petite Fille Sage; Le Herisson)
        Choir of Mary Baldwin College
        Gordon Page, cond.
        *Richmond Sound Stage 10725

        (complete)
        The Tudor Singers of Montreal
        Wayne Riddell, cond.
        CBC Transcription SM-86

PRAETORIUS, Michael (1571-1621)
    Allein Gott in der Hoeh sei Ehr
        Boys Voices of St. Alban's Abbey Choir
        Angel S-37091

Aus tiefer Not schrei ich zu dir
    Boys Voices of St. Alban's Abbey Choir
    Angel S-37091

Christus der uns selig macht
    Boys Voices of St. Alban's Abbey Choir
    Angel S-37091

Erhalt uns, Herr, bei deinem Wort
    Boys Voices of St. Alban's Abbey Choir
    Angel S-37091

Gott der Vater wohn uns bei
    Boys Voices of St. Alban's Abbey Choir
    Angel S-37091

Let Us Chant
    The Tapiola Choir
    Erkki Pohjola, cond.
    Topiolan Joulu 2 -- Qualiton BIS LP 132

Lo, How A Rose
    Mississippi University for Women Chapel Choir
    Marilyn Swingle, dir.
    *

    The Sullins Choir
    Leon B. Fleming, Jr., dir.
    Recorded Publications ErQL2071 (1953-1954)

    Wells College Choir
    Crawford R. Thoburn, dir.
    *(1979-80)

In Natali Domini
    Wells College Choir
    Crawford R. Thoburn, dir.
    *(1980-81)

Psallite Unigenito
    Wells College Choir
    Crawford R. Thoburn, dir.
    *(1980-81)

Resonet in laudibus
    Boys Voices of St. Alban's Abbey Choir
    Angel S-37091

PREUS, Solveig D.
    Haste Not! Rest Not!
        Wheelock College Glee Club
        *Vogts Quality Recording

PRICE
        The Shepherds and The Angels
                Salem Academy Glee Club
                Jean Burroughs, dir.
                *(1980-81) -- Recorded Publications Z-577041

PROKOFIEV, Serge (1891-1953)
        Winter Bonfire, Op. 122
                Prague Radio Children's Chorus & Orchestra
                Alois Klima, cond.
                Supraphon 50.773

PROULX, Richard
        Festival Psalm for a Festival
                School Sisters of St. Francis
                Sister Marie Gnader, dir.
                *Rhapsody of Praise (St. Joseph Convent)

        Happy Is The Man Who Fears The Lord
                Cincinnati BoysChoir
                William Dickinson, dir.
                *The Cincinnati All-City Boychoir

PUCCINI, Giacomo (1858-1924)
        Humming Chorus from "Madame Butterfly"
                Mormon Tabernacle Choir
                Richard T. Condie, cond.
                Favorite Opera Choruses -- Columbia MS 7061

                Roger Wagner Chorale
                Roger Wagner, cond.
                Starlight Chorale: famous Choruses from the Opera --
                        Capitol P 8390

PURCELL, Henry (1659-1695)
        Hymn For Ascensiontide
                London Oratory Junior Choir
                John Hoban, dir.
                Abbey MVP 782

        In These Delightful Pleasant Groves
                Chorale Ensemble of Salem College
                Paul Peterson, dir.
                *The Choral Ensemble of Salem College In Concert --
                        XTV 62399

Sound The Trumpet (Come Ye Sons Of Art Away)
Cincinnati BoysChoir
William Dickinson, dir.
*Cincinnati Boychoir Plays Nashville

Christ's Hospital Singers
Malcolm McKelvey, dir.
Wealden WS 178

Shenandoah Chorus
Robert McSpadden, cond.
*Virginia Music Camp Festival Chorus 1966 -- Custom
Stereo V 25575-3

PURVIS, R.
What Strangers Are These?
Salem Academy Glee Club
Jean Burroughs, dir.
*(1978-1979) -- Recorded Publications Z 530071

PUTRO, Mooses (1848-1919)
Prayer
The Tapiola Choir
Erkki Pohjola, cond.
Songs Of Finland -- Qualiton BIS LP 94

PYCARD (15th c.)
Gloria "Spiritus et Alme"
Women of Columbia University Collegium Musicum
Richard Taruskin, dir.
Music of the Henrys of England -- Collegium Records
JE 119A

RAKSIN, David (1912-   )
Laura
Salem College Choral Ensemble
Paul Peterson, dir.
*On The Campus and On The Road -- CM LP 1006

RAUTAVAARA, Einojuhani (1928-   )
Children's Mass for choir & orchestra
The Tapiola Choir
Erkki Pohjola, dir.
Sounds of Finland -- Qualiton BIS LP 94

Marjatta
The Tapiola Choir
Erkki Pohjola, dir.
Tapiola Joulu 2 -- Qualiton BIS LP 132

Song Cycle to Poems of Frederico Garcia Lorca (contents:
     1. Rider's Song; 2. The Scream; 3. The Moon Peeps
     Out; 4. Dance from Malaga)
  The Tapiola Choir
  Erkki Pohjola, dir.
  Finlandia FA 327

RAVENELLO, Oreste (1871-1938)
  Jesu Redemptor omnium
    Philomela
    Susan Ames-Zierman, dir.
    Make We Joy -- PR 001

REGER, Max (1873-1916)
  Three Songs, Op. 111b
    Stuttgart Women's Chamber Choir
    Frieder Bernius, cond.
    MHS 3449 (1976)

REID, Eric (1936-1970)
  Te Deum
    Choir and School of S. Mary and S. Anne
    Llywela Harris, dir.
    Abbey LPB 668

RHEA
  Evening
    Clovis High School Women's Choir
    Wayne Anderson, dir.
    *Contest Selections - 1981

RIBARY, Antal (1924-   )
  Two Female Choruses (1976) (Contents: Lullaby; The Mirabeau
     Bridge)
    Szilagyi Erzebet Female Choir
    Maria M. Katanies, cond.
    Hungaroton SLPX 12177

RICHTER, Willy
  The Creation
    Lyons Township High School Treble Choir
    Lynne Bradley, dir.
    *(1977) -- Delta DRS 77M 621

RIDOUT, Alan (1934-   )
  Magnificat
    Boys of National Cathedral, Washington, D.C.
    Richard Dirksen, dir.
    *Laudate Dominum -- CAR 009

Sacred Songs, Set II
    Canterbury Cathedral Choir
    Allan Wicks, dir.
    Canterbury Cathedral Choir Sings -- Abbey APR 640

Sacred Songs, Set III
    Guildford Cathedral Choir
    Barry Rose, dir.
    Creator Spirit -- Guild Records

RIMSKY-KORSAKOV, Nicolas (1844-1908)
    Bird Song (Chant de Oiseaux) from Snow Maiden
        Rotterdam Womens Chorus
        David Zinman, cond.
        Philips 6514 306

ROBBINS
    Look Upon The Rainbow
        Lyons Township High School Treble Choir
        Lynne Bradley, dir.
        *(1979) -- Delta DRS 79M 614

RODGERS, Richard (1902-1979)
    Climb Every Mountain (Sound of Music)
        Salem College Choral Ensemble
        Paul W. Peterson, dir.
        *On The Campus and On The Road -- CMLP 1006

    Flower Drum Song (medley)
        Salem Academy Glee Club
        Jean Burroughs, dir.
        *(1978-79) -- Recorded Publications Z 530071

    It's A Grand Night for Singing
        The Sullins Choir
        Leon B. Fleming, Jr., dir.
        Recorded Publications E4QL2071 (1953-54)

    You'll Never Walk Alone
        The Sullins Choir
        Leon B. Fleming, Jr., dir.
        Recorded Publications E4QL2071 (1953-1954)

ROE, Betty (1930-   )
    Prefabulous animiles
        Colet Court Boys Choir
        Ian T. Hunter, cond.
        Pearl SHE 542 (1977)

ROSENMULLER, Johann (1619-1684)
        Lieber Herre Gott
                The Collegium Sagittarii
                Derek McUlloch, dir.
                Oryz EXP 26

ROSS, Henry
        Hail Mary
                Boys' Choir of St. Mary's Hall, Stonyhurst
                Harry Duckworth, dir.
                Carols from St. Mary's Hall, Stonyhurst -- Alpha
                        APS 348

ROSSINI, Gioacchimo (1792-1868)
        Elia Mater (Stabat Mater)
                Rockland County Choral Society
                Philip Hagemann, cond.
                *Crest E-ACDA-80-6B

        Maria Dolcissima
                Swanhurst Choral Society
                Walter Keith, cond.
                MRF 62 (1970)

        The Night Of Holy Christmas (selections: from The Sins Of
                My Old Age)
                Women's Chorus of Lugano Chamber Society
                Nonesuch 71089

ROSZA, Miklos (1907-   )
        Snow Is Falling
                Budapest Children's Choir
                Laszlo Czanyi, cond.
                The Budapest Children's Choir at Carnegie Hall --
                        Victor LM 2861 (1966)

RUBBRA, Edmund (1901-   )
        Autumn, Op. 99
                B.B.C. Women's Chorus
                P. Gellhorn, cond.
                British Institute of Recorded Sound M 3036W

        The Beatitudes, Op. 109
                B.B.C. Women's Chorus
                P. Gellhorn, cond.
                British Institute of Recorded Sound M 3036W

        Missa Brevis, Op. 137
                Trinity Boys Choir, Croydon
                B. Wordsworth, cond.
                British Institute Of Recorded Sound M-2059

A Spring Carol Sequence, Op. 120
    B.B.C. Women's Chorus
    P. Gellhorn, cond.
    British Institute of Recorded Sound M 4900W

RUSSELL, Carlton
    Blessed Be The Lord God
        Wells College Choir
        Crawford R. Thoburn, dir.
        *(1979-80)

    Missa Brevis (1980)
        Wells College Choir
        Crawford R. Thoburn, dir.
        *(1979-80)

RUTTER, John
    For The Beauty Of The Earth
        South Houston Girls Choir
        Sally Schott, dir.
        *Crest ACD-81-2B

    In Dulci Jubilo (arr.)
        Cheltenham Ladies' College Choir
        Dorothy Dickinson, dir.
        Cantique -- Alpha APS 321

    Infant King, The (arr.)
        Boys' Choir of St. Mary's Hall, Stonyhurst
        Harry Duckworth, dir.
        Carols from St. Mary's Hall, Stonyhurst -- Alpha
            APS 348

    Star Carol
        Cheltenham Ladies' College Choir
        Dorothy Dickinson, dir.
        Cantique -- Alph APS 321

SAAR, Victor (arr.)
    Gai l'on la, gai le rosia
        The Aeolian Singers
        Claire Wall, dir.
        *The Impossible Dream Come True

SALLINEN, Aulis (1935-   )
    Ala Tuule Tytti Tuuli
        The Tapiola Choir
        Erkki Pohjola, cond.
        Deutsche Gramophon 2530.812

Balladi
      The Tapiola Choir
      Erkki Pohjola, cond.
      Deutsche Gramophon 2530.812

En mina merytta Kitta
      The Tapiola Choir
      Erkki Pohjola, cond.
      Deutsche Gramophon 2530.812

In Folk Song Style
      The Tapiola Choir
      Erkki Pohjola, cond.
      Finlandia Fa 327

Kieliopillinen Sarja (Suite Grammaticale)
      The Tapiola Choir
      Erkki Pohjola, cond.
      Sounds of Tapiola -- Columbia 5.E-062-34670

Sukura (traditional Japanese folk song)
      The Tapiola Choir
      Erkki Pohjola, cond.
      Sounds of Finland -- Qualiton BIS LP 94

Songs From The Sea (Contents: 1. Wind girl, do not blow;
            2. The Seashape; 3. I don't Praise the Sea;
            4. Fare thee well, my Darling)
      The Tapiola Choir
      Erkki Pohjola, cond.
      Finlandia FA 327

Sympaatti
      Hungarian Radio Children's Choir
      Botka & Csanyi, conds.
      Hungaroton SLPX 12163

      The Tapiola Choir
      Erkki Pohjola, cond.
      Deutsche Gramophon 2530.812

The Winter Was Hard
      The Tapiola Choir
      Erkki Pohjola, cond.
      Sounds of Finland -- Qualiton BIS LP-94

SANDERS, John
   Te Deum
         Cheltenham Ladies' College Choir
         Dorothy Dickinson, dir.
         Alpha ACA 519

When Jesus Christ Was Born
        Cheltenham Ladies' College Choir
        Dorothy Dickinson, dir.
        Cantique -- Alpha APS 321

SANDIG, Hans
    A Small Pony
        Hungarian Radio Children's Chorus
        Botka & Csanyi, cond.
        Hungaroton SLPX 12163

SARGENT, Malcolm (1895-1967)
    Earth's Joys (arr.)
        Choir of S. Mary & S. Anne
        Llywela Harris, dir.
        Ave Maria: A Celebration of Carols -- Alpha APS 315

SARKOSKY, Istavan (1920-   )
    Julia enchek (Julia Songs) (movement 2-Andantina for Tenor
            and Treble Choir)
        Berlin Radio Choir
        Helmut Koch, cond.
        Qualiton LP 1089

SATERN, Leland B. (1913-   )
    We Praise Thee, O God
        Bethel College Women's Choir
        Mary Fall, cond.
        *(1976)

SCHICKELE, Peter (1935-   )
    I Sing Of A Maiden
        University Treble Choir (Illinois State University)
        Donald Armstrong, cond.
        *A Choral Christmas

SCHMIDT, Harvey and Tom Jones
    Fantasticks medley
        Salem Academy Glee Club
        Jean Burroughs, dir.
        *(1980-81) -- Recorded Publications Z 577041

    Try to Remember (from Fantasticks)
        St. Paul's Cathedral Boys Choir
        Rejoice -- K-Tel NE-1064

SCHMITT,
    La tragedie de Salome, Op. 50
        ORTF Girls Choir
        Jean Martinon, cond.
        HMV ASD 2892

SCHOENBERG, Arnold (1872-1951)
  Five Songs from Opus 35 (Hemmung, Das Gesetz, Ausdrucksweise,
     Gluck, Verbundenheit)
    The University of Southern California Dorians
    Michael Ingham, cond.
    *A Program of Music for Women's Voices from the 20th
     Century -- AEA 1094

SCHOUTEN, Joop
  En liten gosse fodder
    Brigittasnstrarnas Klosterkor
    N. deGoede, dir.
    Rosa Rorans Bonitatem -- Proprius PROP 7730

SCHUBERT, Franz (1797-1828)
  Ave Maria
    Columbus Boychoir
    Herbert Huffman, cond.
    Festival of Song -- Decca DL 8106

  Chor der Engel (D.440)
    Elizabethan Singers
    Louis Halsey, cond.
    Argo ZRG 527

  Gebet (D.815)
    Elizabethan Singers
    Louis Halsey, cond.
    Argo ZRG 527

  German Dances
    Vienna Choir Boys
    Romantic Vienna -- Everest SDBR 3240

  Glory To God
    Bethel College Women's Choir
    Oliver Mogck, dir.
    *(1972)

  Der Gondelfahre (D.809)
    Elizabethan Singers
    Louis Halsey, cond.
    Argo ZRG 527

  Gott in der Natur, Op. 133 (D757)
    Elizabethan Singers
    Louis Halsey, cond.
    Argo ZRG 527

    Stuttgart Vocal Ensemble
    Marcel Couraud, cond.
    Discophile francais DF 442

Gott in Ungewitter (D.985)
 Elizabethan Singers
 Louis Halsey, cond.
 Argo ZRG 527

Gott, mein Zuversicht, Op. 132 (D.706)
 Elizabethan Singers
 Louis Halsey, cond.
 Argo ZRG 527

 St. Hedwig's Cathedral Choir
 Karl Forster, cond.
 Electrola SMVP 8043

 Stuttgart Vocal Ensemble
 Marcel Couraud, cond.
 Discophile francais DF 142

 Vienna Choir Boys
 Hans Gillesberger, dir.
 Vienna Choir Boys Serenade -- RCA PRL 1-9034

Das Grosse Hallelujah
 Miami Boy Choir
 Paul A. Eisenhart, cond.
 *Crest S-ACDA-80-4B

The Lord Is My Shepherd
 Choir and School of S. Mary and S. Anne
 Llywela Harris, dir.
 In Quires and Places #5 -- Abbey LPB 668; also Day By
  Day -- Argo ZRG 785

 East Carolina University Women's Glee Club
 Rhonda Fleming, dir.
 *HIS Recording

 Choristers of Worcester Cathedral
 Abbey LPB 764 (1976)

Die Nachtigall, Op. 11, #2 (D.724)
 Vienna Choir Boys
 Hans Gillesberger, dir.
 Vienna Choir Boys Serenade -- RCA PRL 1-9034

Nachthelle, Op. 134 (D.892)
 Elizabethan Singers
 Louis Halsey, cond.
 Argo ZRG 527

 Musica Aeterna Chamber Chorus
 Decca DL 79437

La Pastorella, (D. 513)
    Vienna Choir Boys
    Hans Gillesberger, dir.
    Vienna Choir Boys Serenade -- RCA PRL 1-9034

Sanctus (from German Mass)
    Alabama Music Educators All State
    Hugh Thomas, dir.
    Alabama Music Educators All State Grand Concert --
        USC Sound Enterprise

    Vienna Choir Boys
    Romantic Vienna -- Everest SDBR 3240

Standchen, Op. 135 (D.921)
    Choir of the Bavarian Staatsoper, Munich
    Wolfgang Baumgart, cond.
    Lieder von Franz Schubert -- EMI C-065-28-969

    Elizabethan Singers
    Louis Halsey, cond.
    Argo ZRG 527

    Lyons Township High School Treble Choir
    Lynne Bradley, dir.
    *(1978) -- Delta DRS 78M 720A

    Musica Aeterna Chamber Chorus
    Decca DL 79437

    Vienna Choir Boys
    Hans Gilleberger, dir.
    Vienna Choir Boys Serenade -- RCA PRL 1-9034

    Vienna Choir Boys
    Robert Kihbacher, dir.
    Epis LC 3648

The Trout
    Vienna Choir Boys
    Romantic Vienna - Everest SDBR 3240

Widerspruch, Op. 105 (D. 865)
    Vienna Choir Boys
    Hans Gillesberger, dir.
    Vienna Choir Boys Serenade -- RCA PR1 1-9034

SCHUMAN, William (1910-)
    Concerto on Old English Rounds
        Camarata Singers
        Leonard Bernstein & New York Philharmonic
        Columbia M35101 (1978)

Requiescat
    Choir of Mary Baldwin College
    Gordon Page, dir.
    *Richmond Sound Stage 10725

    University of North Carolina Choir
    Richard Cox, dir.
    *Twentieth Century Compositions for Treble Voices --
        CSS 554

SCHUMANN, Robert (1810-1856)
    Dreaming Lake
        Budapest Children's Choir
        Laszlo Czanyi, cond.
        The Budapest Children's Choir at Carnegie Hall --
            Victor LM 2861 (1966)

    Gesange fur Frauenstimme
        University of Georgia Women's Glee Club
        Ann H. Jones, cond.
        *Crest S-ACDA-80-3A

    Jager wohlgemat, Op. 91, #2
        Berlin Radio Choir
        Helmut Koch, cond.
        Qualiton LP 1089

    Romances, Book I, Op. 69 (Contents: 1. Tamburin schlagerin;
            2. Waldmadchen; 3. Klosterfraulein;
            4. Soldatenbraut; 5. Meerfrey; 6. Die Capelle)
        Kodaly Girls Choir
        Ilona Andor, cond.
        Hungaroton SLPX 11-862

        Stuttgart Kammerchor
        Frieder Bernius, cond.
        EMI 1C 065 30807 (1978)

        Stuttgart Pro Musica Choir
        Marcel Couraud, cond.
        Discophiles francais DF 192

    Romances, Book II, Op. 91 (Contents: 7. Rosmarien; 8. Jager
            Wohlgemuth; 9. Der Wassermann; 10. Der Verlassene
            Magdlein; 11. Der Bleicherin Nachtlied;
            12. In Meeres Mitten)
        Kodaly Girls Choir
        Ilona Andor, cond.
        Hungaroton SLPX 11-862

        Stuttgart Vocal Ensemble
        Marcel Couraud, cond.
        Discophiles francais DF 192

Rosmarien, Op. 91, #1
    Berlin Radio Choir
    Helmut Koch, cond.
    Qualiton LP 1089

Tamburinschlagerin, Op. 69, #1
    Berlin Radio Choir
    Helmut Koch, cond.
    Qualiton LP 1089

Zigeunerleben, Op. 29, #3
    Vienna Choir Boys
    Hans Gillesberger, dir.
    Vienna Choir Boys Serenade -- RCA PRL 1-9034

SCHUTZ, Heinrich (1585-1672)
    Bring her den Herren, ihr Gewaltigen (SWV 283) (Kleine
            Geistliche Konzerte, Bk I)
        Westphalian Choral Ensemble
        Wilhelm Ehmann, dir.
        Nonesuch HB 73012

    Der Herr ist Gross und sehr Loeblich (SWV 286) (Kleine
            Geistliche Konzerte, Bk I)
        Westphalian Choral Ensemble
        Wilhelm Ehmann, dir.
        Nonesuch HB 73012

    Eile, mich, Gott, zu erretten (SWV 282) (Kleine Geistliche
            Konzerte, Bk I)
        Westphalian Choral Ensemble
        Wilhelm Ehmann, dir.
        Nonesuch HB 73012

    Erhore mich, wenn ich rufe (SWV 289) (Kleine Geistliche
            Konzerte, Bk I)
        Westphalian Choral Ensemble
        Wilhelm Ehmann, dir.
        Nonesuch HB 73012

    Give Ear O Lord
        Salem College Choral Ensemble
        Paul W. Peterson, dir.
        *On The Campus and On The Road
            CMLP 1006

Habe deine Lust an dem Herren (Kleine Geistliche Konzerte)
    Gregg Smith Singers
    Gregg Smith, cond.
    Vox SVBX 5103

Ich danke dem Herrn von ganzern Herzen, im Rat der Frommen
    (SWV 284) (Kleine Geistliche Konzerte, Bk I)
    Westphalian Choral Ensemble
    Wilhelm Ehmann, dir.
    Nonesuch HB 73012

Ihr Heiligen, lobsinget dem Herren (SWV 288) (Kleine
    Geistliche Konzerte, Bk I)
    Westphalian Choral Ensemble
    Wilhelm Ehmann, dir.
    Nonesuch HB 73012

Liebster, sagt in suessen Schmerzen
    Gregg Smith Singers
    Gregg Smith, cond.
    Vox SVBX 5103

Lobet den Herren, der zu Zion wohnet (SWV 293) (Kleine
    Geistliche Konzerte, Bk I)
    Westphalian Choral Ensemble
    Wilhelm Ehmann, dir.
    Nonesuch HB 73012

O hilf Christi, Gottes Sohn (Kleine Geistliche Konzerte)
    Gregg Smith Singers
    Gregg Smith, dir.
    Vox SVBX 5013

O lieber Herre Gott, Wecke uns auf (SWV 237) (Kleine
    Geistliche Konzerte, Bk I)
    Westphalian Choral Ensemble
    Wilhelm Ehmann, dir.
    Nonesuch HB 73012

Tugend ist der bester Freund
    Gregg Smith Singers
    Gregg Smith, dir.
    Vox SVBX 5103

Wohl dem, der nicht wandelt in Rat der Gottlosen
    (SWV 290) (Kleine Geistliche Konzerte)
    Westphalian Choral Ensemble
    Wilhelm Ehmann, dir.
    Nonesuch HB 73012

SCOTTISH FOLK SONG
      Coulters Candy (arr. DeCormier)
            The Aeolian Singers
            Claire Wall, dir.
            *The Impossible Dream Comes True

      Dream agnus (arr. Phillips)
            The Aeolian Singers
            Claire Wall, dir.
            *The Impossible Dream Comes True

SEIBER, Matyas (1903-1960)
      Hungarian Folk Songs (Handsome Butcher; Apple, Apple)
            Choir and School of S. Mary and S. Anne
            In Quires and Places, #5 -- Abbey LPB 668

SHAW, Kirby
      Girl Talk
            Lyons Township High School Treble Choir
            Lynne Bradley, dir.
            *Friends -- Delta DRS 81M-105

SHAW, Martin (1875-1958)
      A Blessing
            Mississippi University for Women Chapel Choir
            Marilyn Swingle, dir.
            *

            Salem College Choral Ensemble
            Paul W. Peterson, dir.
            *On The Campus and On The Road -- CMLP 1006

      Go Forth Into The World In Peace (arr. Jacobson)
            Bethel College Women's Choir
            Oliver Mogck, dir.
            *Gold Cover

      With A Voice of Singing
            The Sullins Choir
            Leon B. Fleming, Jr., dir.
            Recorded Publications E41L2071 (1953-1954)

SHIMMIN, Sydney
      White, Blue and Gold
            Chalentenham Ladies' College Choir
            Dorothy Dickinson, dir.
            Cantique -- Alpha APS 321

SIBELIUS, Jean (1865-1957)
    Finlandia
        Lyons Township High School Treble Choir
        Lynne Bradley, dir.
        *(1975) -- Delta DRS 75-423

        The Tapiola Choir
        Erkki Pohjola, cond.
        Songs of Finland -- Qualiton BIS LP 94; Finlandia
            FA 327

    Onward Ye People
        The Salem Academy Glee Club
        Jean Burroughs, dir.
        *(1980-81) -- Recorded Publications Z 577041

    Song Of My Heart
        The Tapiola Choir
        Erkki Pohjola, cond.
        Songs of Finland -- Qualiton BIS LP 94

    Song of Peace (Finlandia)
        Lyons Township High School Treble Choir
        Lynne Bradley, dir.
        *Friends -- Delta DRS 81M 105

    The Snow Is Falling
        The Tapiola Choir
        Erkki Pohjola, cond.
        Tapiolan Joulu 2 -- Qualiton BIS LP 132

SICILIAN TUNE
    Sicilian Bagpiper's Carol (arr. K.K. Davis)
        Philomela
        Susan Ames-Zierman, dir.
        Make We Joy -- PR 001

SILVER, Frederick (1936-   )
    Twelve Days After Christmas
        The Salem Academy Glee Club
        Jean Burroughs, dir.
        *(1978-79) -- Recorded Publications Z-530071

SIMEONE, H. (arr.) (1911-   )
    Anthem For Spring (Cavalleria Rusticana)
        Lyons Township High School Treble Choir
        Lynne Bradley, dir.
        *(1979) -- Delta DRS 79M 614

SING CHILDREN SING
        (A collection of folk songs: Uncle Sam's Farm; Go Tell
                Aunt Rhody; Meshivotzi no-otz; Ol' Dan Tucker;
                Shenandoah; The Singing School; Wayfaring
                Stranger; The Blue Tail Fly; Gentle Annie;
                Great Grandad; The Farmer Is The Man; The Erie
                Canal; Simple Gifts; Stars Shining By and By)
        New York City Opera Children's Chorus
        Robert DeCromier, arr. & cond.
        Caedmon TC 1558 (1977)

SIRCOM, Eunice (arr.)
    The Old Man
        The Aeolian Singers
        Claire Wall, dir.
        *The Impossible Dream Comes True

SLEETH, Natalie
    Gaudeamus Hodie
        Cincinnati BoysChoir
        William Dickinson, dir.
        *Cincinnati All City Boychoir

SLESSOR, T.
    De Virgin Mary (arr.)
        Choir of S. Mary & S. Anne
        Llywela Harris, dir.
        Ave Maria: A Celebration of Carols -- Alpha APS 315

SMALIS
    If You Believe (The Wiz) (arr. Ringwald)
        Lyons Township High School Treble Choir
        Lynne Bradley, dir.
        *Friends -- Delta DRS 81M-105

SMART, Henry
    The Lord Is My Shepherd
        Boys' Choir of St. Mary's Hall, Stonyhurst
        Pueri Sanctae Mariae -- Alpha APS 322

SMETENA, Bedrich (1824-1884)
    My Star
        Czech Philharmonic Chorus
        Josef Veselka, cond.
        Supraphon 1-12-1143 (1973)

    Spring Chorus from Bartered Bride
        Lyons Township High School Treble Choir
        Lynne Bradley, dir.
        *Laudate Pueri Dominum a due Chori -- Delta DRS 78M
            720A

The Sunset
    Czech Philharmonic Chorus
    Josef Veselka, cond.
    Supraphon 1-12-1143 (1973)

The Swallows
    Czech Philharmonic Chorus
    Josef Veselka, cond.
    Supraphon 1-12-1143 (1973)

Three Choruses for Women's Voices (Tri Zenske Sbory)
        (1. My Star-Ma Hvezda; 2. The Swallows Arrived-
        Priletely Viastovicky; 3. The Sunset-Za hory
        slunce zapada)
    Czech Philharmonic Chorus
    Josef Veselka, cond.
    Supraphon 1-12-1143 (1973)

    Lyons Township High School Treble Choir
    Lynne Bradley, dir.
    *Crest NC-ACD-80-6A

SMITH, Alexander Brent
    Come My Way (arr. Dorothy Dickinson)
        Cheltenham Ladies' College Choir
        Dorothy Dickinson, dir.
        Cantique -- Alpha APS 321

SMITH, Gregg (1931-   )
    Beware of the Soldier (1969)
        Texas Boys Choir
        George Bragg, cond.
        CRI 3-341

    Bible Songs for Young Voices
        Miami Boy Choir
        Paul A. Eisenhart, dir.
        *Crest ACD 81-3B; Turnabout 34544 (Cassette 2218)

        Texas Boys Choir
        Gregg Smith, dir.
        Turnabout 34544

SMITH, Melville
    Lully, Lullay
        University Treble Choir (Illinois State University)
        Donald Armstrong, cond.
        *

SOLIVA, Carlo (1792-1851)
    Ave Maria
        Coro femminile della Radio svizezra italian
        Edwin Loehrer, cond.
        Communaute de travail pou la diffusion de la musique
            suisse STC 32 (1967)

SOUTHERN FOLK TUNE
    When Jesus Left His Father's Throne (arr. David Johnson)
        Bethel College Women's Choir
        Oliver Mogck, dir.
        *Gold Cover

SOWERBY, Leo (1895-1968)
    Behold What Manners of Love
        Bethel College Women's Choir
        Oliver Mogck, dir.
        *Gold Cover

SPANISH CAROL
    A la nanita nana
        Philomela
        Susan Ames-Zierman, dir.
        Make We Joy -- PR 001

    El cant dels ocells
        Philomela
        Susan Ames-Zierman, dir.
        Make We Joy -- PR 001

    Riu, riu, chiu
        Philomela
        Susan Ames-Zierman, dir.
        Make We Joy -- PR 001

SPENCER
    Angelus Ad Virginem
        University of Virginia Women's Chorus
        Katherine Mitchell, dir.
        *Candlelight Christmas -- 8393

SPIRITUAL
    Ezekiel Saw De Wheel (arr. Noble Cain)
        Bethel College Women's Choir
        Oliver Mogck, dir.
        *Gold Cover

    Go Tell It On The Mountain
        The Tapiola Choir
        Erkki Pohjola, cond.
        Deutsche Gramophon Z530.812; Sounds of Tapiola --
            Columbia 5.E-062-34670

    Oh Peter, Go Ring Them Bells (arr. Carl-Bertil Agnestig)
        The Tapiola Choir
        Erkki Pohjola, cond.
        Deutsche Gramophon Z530-812

O Mary, Don't You Weep (arr. C.E. Thomas)
    Bethel College Women's Choir
    Mary Fall, dir.
    *(1979)

Rise! Shine! (arr. Carl Parrish)
    Bethel College Women's Chorus
    Oliver Mogck, dir.
    *(1972)

    Smith College Chamber Singers
    Iva Dee Hiatt, cond.
    First International University Choral Festival --
        RCA LSC 7043

Sometimes I Feel Like A Motherless Child (arr. C.E. Thomas)
    Bethel College Women's Choir
    Mary Fall, cond.
    *(1979)

Standin' in de Need Of Prayer (arr. Brian Trent)
    Choir and School of S. Mary and S. Anne
    Llywela Harris, dir.
    In Quires and Places, #5 -- Abbey LPB 668

There Is A Balm In Gilead (arr. Theron Kirk)
    Mississippi University for Women Chapel Choir
    Marilyn Swingle, dir.
    *

Were You There (arr. Burleigh)
    Salem College Choral Ensemble
    Paul W. Peterson, dir.
    *On The Campus and On The Road -- CMLP 1006

Who Is That Yonder (arr. Russell Woolen)
    Bethel College Women's Choir
    Mary Fall, dir.
    *

STANFORD, Charles Villiers (1852-1924)
    Te Deum in B-flat
        Choir of the School of St. Mary & St. Anne
        Llywela Harris, dir.
        Day By Day -- Argo ZRG 785

STERN, Robert (1934-   )
    Three Chinese Poems (1970-1971)
        Women's Voices of the University Chorale of Indiana
            University
        Alan Harler, cond.
        Advance FGR 24S (1978)

STEVENS, Halsey (1908-   )
    O Sing Unto The Lord A New Song (Psalm 98) (1955)
        Mid-American Chorale
        John Dexter, dir.
        Sing Unto The Lord A New Song -- Composers Recordings
            CRI 191

        Wheaton College Women's Chorale
        Mary Hopper, dir.
        *Let All The World In Every Corner Sing -- WETN 820-501

STOCKER, David
    Festival Responses
        Bethel College Women's Choir
        Mary Fall, dir.
        *(1976)

        Lyons Township High School Treble Choir
        Lynne Bradley, dir.
        *Crest NC-ACDA-80-6A; *Patterns in Music -- Delta
            DRS 74-139A

        Wheaton College Women's Chorale
        Mary Hopper, cond.
        *Let All The World In Every Corner Sing -- WETN 820-501

STRATEGIER, Herman
    Cantica pro tempore natali (2nd motet for SSAA)
        Netherlands Chamber Choir
        Felix de Noble, cond.
        Donemus DAVS 6104 (1961)

STRAUSS, Johann
    Nun's Chorus (from Casanova) (arr. Ralph Benatsky)
        Philharmonia Orchestra and Chorus
        Otto Ackermann, cond.
        Elizabeth Schwarzkopf Sings Operetta -- Angel S-35696

STRAVINSKY, Igor (1892-1971)
    Cantata (1952)
        Czech Philharmonic Chorus & Orchestra
        Karel Ancerl, cond.
        Supraphon SUA ST 59078 (1968)

        English Chamber Orchestra & Choir
        L'oiseau-Lyre OL 265 (SD SOL 265)

        Frauenchor von St. Lorenz, Nurnburg
        Herman Harrasowitz, cond.
        BR Nurnburg 181988 (1970)

Cantata (1952) (continued)
    Gregg Smith Singers
    Igor Stravinsky, cond.
    Columbia MS 6992

    Members of the New York Concert Choir
    Igor Stravinsky, cond.
    Columbia ML 4899

    Choir and Orchestra of Tschechischen Philharmonie
    Ancerl, cond.

Four Russian Peasant Folksongs
    Gregg Smith Singers
    Gregg Smith, cond.
    Columbia M-31124

    Los Ninos Cantores De Puebla -- Classic Pick
        70-114 (1975)

    Paris Opera Women's Chorus
    Pierre Boulez, cond.
    Nonesuch 71133 (1966)

    (Un-named chorus)
    Igor Stravinsky, cond.
    Columbia ML 5107

    University of Southern California Dorians
    Michael Ingham, cond.
    *A Program of Music for Women's Voices from the 20th
        Century -- AEA 1094

STROUSE, Charles (1928-   )
    Annie (from Annie) (arr. Simeone)
        Lyons Township High School Treble Choir
        Lynne Bradley, dir.
        *Laudate Pueri Dominum a due Cori -- Delta DRS 48M;
            *Bursting Out -- Delta DRS 82M 116

    You're Never Fully Dressed Without A Smile (Annie)
            (arr. Metis)
        Lyons Township High School Treble Choir
        Lynne Bradley, dir.
        *Laudate Pueri Dominum a due Cori -- Delta DRS 78M

SUMSION, Herbert (1899-   )
    Watt's Cradle Song
        Gloucester Cathedral Choir
        John Sanders, dir.
        Carols For Christmas -- Abbey MVP 807 (1979)

TALLIS, Thomas (1505-1585)
        Heare The Voyce and Prayer of Thy Servants
                South Houston Girls Choir
                Sally Schott, dir.
                *Crest ACD-81-2B

        If Ye Love Me (arr. Thoburn)
                Wells College Choir
                Crawford R. Thoburn, dir.
                *(1979-80)

TCHAIKOVSKY, Peter I. (1840-1893)
        Andante Cantabile
                Peninsula Women's Chorus
                Patricia Hennings, dir.
                *Song of Survival

        The Legend
                Columbus Boychoir
                Herbert Huffman, dir.
                Festival of Song -- Decca DL 8136

THIMAN, Eric (1900-1975)
        Jesus Lives!
                Bethel College Women's Choir
                Oliver Mogck, dir.
                *Gold Cover

        Seasonal Thanksgiving, A
                Mississippi University for Women Chapel Choir
                Marilyn Swingle, dir.
                *

THOMPSON, Randall (1899-1984)
        A Girl's Garden (Frostiana)
                Radcliffe Choral Society
                Randall Thompson, cond.
                *Harvard Glee Club FH-RT

                The Singing Sargents
                Craig Jessop, dir.
                *The Road Not Taken

        Choose Something Like A Star (Frostiana)
                Holy Cross Convent
                Sister Joan M. Whittemore
                *American Music 1776-1976

        Come In (Frostiana)
                Mary Baldwin College Choir
                Gordon Page, dir.
                *Richmond Sound Stage 10725

Come In (Frostiana) (continued)
        Radcliffe Choral Society
        Randall Thompson, cond.
        *Harvard Glee Club FH-RT

        Singing Sargeants
        Craig D. Jessop, dir.
        *The Road Not Taken

Now I Lay Me Down To Sleep
        Lyons Township High School Treble Choir
        Lynne Bradley, dir.
        *Laudate Pueri Dominum a due Cori -- Delta DRS 78M-720A

The Place Of The Blest
        Glen Ellyn Children's Chorus
        Doreen Rao, cond.
        *Delta/Stereo DRS 76M 536

Pueri Hebraeorum
        Choral Ensemble of Salem College
        Paul Peterson, dir.
        *Choral Ensembles of Salem College in Concert --
            XTV 62399

        Columbus Boy Choir
        Donald Brant, cond.
        Cademon CBC 15

        New Mexico All State Girls Choir
        John D. Raymond, dir.
        *New Mexico Music Educators Association -- Century
            Stereo 29256

        University of North Carolina Choir
        Richard Cox, dir.
        *Twentieth Century Compositions for Treble Voices --
            CSS 554

THOMSON, Virgil (1896-   )
    Mass
        King's Chapel, Boston
        Cambridge 412

TIPTON, Clyde (1934-   )
    Any One Lived In a Pretty How Town
        Lyons Township High School Treble Choir
        Lynne Bradley, dir.
        *Friends -- Delta DRS 81M 104

    I Thank You God
        Lyons Township High School Treble Choir
        Lynne Bradley, dir.
        *(1979) -- Delta DRS 79M 614; *Drest NC-ACDA 80-6A

THYBO, Lief (1922-   )
      Rosa Rorans (Brigitta-hymn - 1973)
            Womens Chorus
            Ostman, dir.
            Caprice RIKS 47

TOMASI, Henri
      Divertisment Pastorale
            Boys of the l'O.R.T.F. Chorus and Orchestra
            Jacques Joineau, cond.
            Deutsche Grammaphon -- 2355-375

TRADITIONAL
      Gabriel's Message (Baring-Gould)
            Choir of the School of St. Mary & St. Anne
            Llywela Harris, dir.
            Day By Day -- Argo ZRG 785

      O Come, O Come Emmanuel
            Chapel Choir of the Blue-Coat School, Birmingham
            Hugh Shelton, dir.
            Abbey LPB 645

      Song Of The Nuns Of Chester
            Chapel Choir of the Blue Coat School, Birmingham
            Hugh Shelton, dir.
            Abbey LPB 645

TRANT, Brian
      O Sleep Thou Heav'n Born Treasure (arr.)
            Choir of S. Mary & S. Anne
            Llywela Harris, dir.
            Ave Maria: A Celebration of Carols -- Alpha APS 315

UKRANIAN CAROL
      Carol Of The Bells
            Philomela
            Susan Ames-Zierman, dir.
            Make We Joy -- PR 001

USENKO, V.
      Gori, Koster
            A. Birchanskii, cond.
            Four Children's Songs by 3 Soviet Composers --
                  (Russian recording-copy at Library of Congress)

VALERIA, Cxanyi
    Jalo, Jalo
        Hungarian Radio Children's Chorus
        Botka & Cxanyi, conds.
        Hongaroton SLPX 12163

VanVLECK, Jacob (1751-1831)
    I Will Rejoice In The Lord (Kroger)
        Lyons Township High School Treble Choir
        Lynne Bradley, dir.
        *Bursting Out -- Delta DRS 82M 116

VAUGHAN-WILLIAMS, Ralph (1872-1958)
    All People Than On Earth Do Dwell
        Cheltenham Ladies' College Choir
        Dorothy Dickinson, dir.
        Cantique -- Alpha APS 321

    Lullabye (from Hodie)
        Wells College Choir
        Crawford R. Thoburn, dir.
        *(1979-80)

    Magnificat
        Women's voices of Ambrosian Singers
        Meredith Davis, cond.
        EMI SLS 5082; Angel 36819 (1972)

        Syracuse Choir
        Desto S-102

        The University Choir
        Richard Cox, dir.
        *Christmas Concert 1964 -- CSS 423-1598A

    Sound Sleep
        The University of North Carolina Choir
        Richard Cox, dir.
        *Twentieth Century Compositions for Treble Voices --
            CSS 554

    To The Ploughboy (from Folk Songs of the Four Seasons)
        Radcliffe Choral Society
        Beverly Taylor, cond.
        AFKA Records SK 4674

    Ye Watchers and Ye Holy Ones
        Chapel Choir of the Blue-Coat School, Birmingham
        Hugh Shelton, dir.
        Abbey LPB 645

VECCHI, Orazio (1550-1605)
    Damon e Filli
        Vassar Madrigal Singers
        E. Harold Geer, cond.
        The Italian Madrigal: Ars Nova and the 16th c. --
            Allegro Records ALG 3029

    Sing Me A Song
        Agnes Scott College Glee Club
        Richard Hensel, dir.
        *Agnes Scott Glee Club Spring Concert 1964

VERDI, Giuseppi (1813-1901)
    Laudi Alla Vergine (from Quattro Pezzi Sacri)
        Chicago Symphony Chorus
        Sir George Solti, cond.
        London 26610

        Choristers of Worcester Cathedral
        Abbey LPB 764 (1976)

        Hilversum Radio Choirs
        Ricardo Muti, cond.
        1974 Holland Festival - Radio Nederlad 6808.323/324

        Los Angeles Master Chorale
        Los Angeles Philharmonic/Mehta
        Decca OS 26176

        Lucerene Vocalsoloists
        Franz Xavier Jan, dir.
        Tudor 73029

        Lyons Township High School Treble Choir
        Lynne Bradley, dir.
        *(1975) -- Delta DRS 75-423

        Maggio Musicale Fiorentino Choir & Orchestra
        Ettore Gracis, cond.
        Deutsche Grammophon LPM 78962; DG Privilege 2538 343

        Musica Aeterna Chorus & Orchestra
        Fredereich Waldman, dir.
        Decca DL 79429

        Philharmonia Orchestra Chorus
        Giulini, cond.
        Angel S-6125

        Radio Chorus & Orchestra of Leipzig
        Herbert Kegel, cond.
        Philips 6570-111 (1971)

Laudi Alla Vergine (continued)
    Salarello Choir
    Bradshaw, cond.
    CRD 1009

    Swedish Radio/Stockholm Chorus
    R. Muti, dir.
    Angel DS 38000 (Digital)

    University Treble Choir (Illinois State University)
    Donald Armstrong, cond.
    *

VERHAALEN, Sister Marion
    Sing To Our God
        School Sisters of St. Francis
        Sister Marie Gnader, dir.
        *Rhapsody of Praise (St. Joseph Convent)

VERNON, Knight
    Haiku West: Magical Nature
        Mississippi University for Women Chapel Choir
        Marilyn Swingle, dir.
        *

VIADANA, Lodovico (1560-1627)
    Laetare Jerusalem
        The London Oratory Junior Choir
        John Hoban, dir.
        Laetare Jerusalem -- Abbey MVP 782

VICTORIA, Tomas de
    O Vos Omnes
        Mississippi University for Women Chapel Choir
        Marilyn Swingle, dir.
        *

        Wells College Choir
        Crawford R. Thoburn, dir.
        *(1979-80)

    O Ye People (SEE: O Vos Omnes)

VIDAL, Paul (1863-1931)
    Chanson des Anges
        University Treble Choir (Illinois State University)
        Donald Armstrong, dir.
        *A Choral Christmas

VILLO-LOBOS, Heitor (1887-1959)
    No Canto orfeonico
        Coro dos Meninos Cantores de Petropolis
        Jose V. Brandao, cond.
        Caravelle LP NF 43.007

Quatuor
    Roger Wagner Chorale
    Roger Wagner, cond.
    Capitol P-8191

The Sewing Girls
    Clovis High School Women's Choir
    Wayne Anderson, dir.
    *

VITTORIA (SEE: VICTORIA, Thomas de)

VIVALDI, Antonio (1678-1741)
    Gloria (selections)
        Salem Academy Glee Club
        Jean Burroughs, dir.
        *(1978-79) -- Recorded Publications Z-530071

    Laudamus Te (Gloria)
        Cincinnati BoysChoir
        William Dickinson, dir.
        *Cincinnati Boychoir Plays Nashville

VULPIUS, Melchior (1570-1615)
    An Easter Hallelujah
        Wheaton College Women's Chorale
        Mary Hopper, cond.
        *Let All The World In Every Corner Sing -- WETN 820-01

    Good Christian Men Rejoice (arr. Ley)
        Chapel Choir of the Blue-Coat School, Birmingham
        Hugh Shelton, dir.
        Abbey LPB 645

    Spring Comes Again
        Clovis High School Treble Tones
        Wayne Anderson, dir.
        *Contest Selections 1981

WAGNER, Richard (1813-1883)
    Jo ho hoel Traft ihr das Schiff (from der Fliegende
            Hollander)
        Frauenchor der Ungarischen Staatsoper
        Ferene Nagy, dir.
        Hungaroton SLPX 11940

WALKER, J. F.
    Clear Vault Of Heaven
        Choir of the School of St. Mary & St. Anne
        Llywela Harris, dir.
        Day By Day -- Argo ZRG 785

WARE, Harriet (1877-1962)
    The Artisan
        Music by Harriet Ware -- L. Sherman (1971)

WASNER, Franz (arr.)
    Bring Your Torches
        Women of Mormon Tabernacle Choir
        Richard Condie, dir.
        The Mormon Tabernacle Choir Greatest Hits Of
            Christmas -- CBS 37853

WATSON, Walter (1933-   )
    Five Japanese Love Poems (1969)
        Kent State University Women's Glee Club
        Clayton Krehbiel, cond.
        Music From Cleveland -- Advent Records USR 5005

WEBSTER-FAIR
    Love Is A Many Splendored Thing
        Salem College Choral Ensemble
        Paul W. Peterson, dir.
        *On The Campus and On The Road -- CMLP 1006

WEELKES, Thomas (1575-1623)
    The Nightingale (Greyson)
        Clovis High School Women's Choir
        Wayne Anderson, dir.
        *

        Lyons Township High School Treble Choir
        Lynne Bradley, dir.
        *Laudate Pueri Dominum a due Cori -- Delta DRS 78M
            720A

        Miami Boychoir
        Paul A. Eisenhart, cond.
        *Crest S-ACDA-80-4B

        Miami Girls Chorus
        Lynne Huff, cond.
        *HIS Recording

        Philomela
        Susan Ames-Zierman, dir.
        Many Butterflies -- RBR 001

    To Shorten Winter's Sadness
        Philomela
        Susan Ames-Zierman, dir.
        Many Butterflies -- RBR 001

Welcome, Sweet Pleasure
        Choir and School of S. Mary and S. Anne
        Llywela Harris, dir.
        In Quires and Places #5 -- Abbey LPB 668

WESLEY, Samuel Sebastian (1810-1876)
    The Church's One Foundation
        Bethel College Women's Choir
        Mary Fall, cond.
        *(1979)

    Who Can Express
        Choristers of Worcester Cathedral
        Abbey LPB 764 (1976)

WESSMAN, Harri
    Waters Weary Under Snow
        The Tapiola Choir
        Erkki Pohjola, dir.
        Finlandia FA 327

WHITE, Jack
    Traveling Musicians
        Hungarian Radio Children's Chorus
        Botka & Csanyi, conds.
        Hungaroton SLPX 12163

WHITE, L. J.
    Prayer of St. Richard of Chicester
        Choir of Rochester Cathedral
        Barry Ferguson, dir.
        Music from Rochester Cathedral -- Abbey APR 302

WHITECOTTON, Shirley (1935-   )
    Flow Not So Fast, Ye Mountains
        Lyons Township High School Treble Choir
        Lynne Bradley, dir.
        *(1979)

    To Live Beautifully
        Lyons Township High School Treble Choir
        Lynne Bradley, dir.
        *(1977)

WILBYE, John (1574-1638)
    Adieu, Sweet Amaryllis
        Choir and School of S. Mary and S. Anne
        Llywela Harris, dir.
        In Quires and Places, #5 -- Abbey LPB 668

    Weep O Mine Eyes
        Agnes Scott College Glee Club
        Richard Hensel, dir.
        *Agnes Scott College Glee Club Spring Concert 1964

WILLAN, Healey (1880-1968)
      Let All The World In Every Corner Sing
            Wheaton College Women's Chorale
            Mary Hopper, dir.
            *Let All The World In Every Corner Sing -- WETN 820-501

      Tyrle, Trylow
            University Treble Choir (Illinois State University)
            Donald Armstrong, cond.
            *A Choral Christmas

WILLS, Arthur (1926-   )
      Ave Verum Corpus
            Choir and School of St. Mary and St. Anne
            Llywela Harris, dir.
            In Quires and Places #5 -- Abbey LPB 668

      Mass of St. Mary and St. Anne
            Choir of the School of St. Mary and St. Anne
            Llywela Harris, dir.
            Day By Day -- Argo ZRG 785

      There Is No Rose
            Durham Cathedral Choir
            Richard Lloyd, dir.
            Carols from Durham Cathedral -- Abbey MVP 800

WINSLOW, Richard (1918-   )
      Recessional
            Wheelock College Glee Club
            Leo Collis, dir.
            *Vogts Quality Recording

WOOLEN, Russell (1923-   )
      Who Is That Yonder
            Bethel College Women's Choir
            Mary Fall, cond.
            *(1976)

WOOD
      Carol from an Irish Cabin
            St. Joseph's Academy
            Sister Joan M. Whittenmore
            *Christmas Record (1978)

      There Stood In Heaven A Linden Tree
            Chapel Choir of the Blue-Coat School, Birmingham
            Hugh Shelton, dir.
            Abbey LPB 645

XENAKIS, Iannis (1922-   )
    Polla ta Dhina (1962)
        Children's Choir of Notre Dame De Paris with Paris
            Instrumental Ensemble for Contemporary Music
        Angel S-36656 (1969)

YAMAMOTO, Naozumi
    Kompira-fune-fune (Japanese folk song from Kagawa province)
        The Tapiola Choir
        Erkki Pohjola, dir.
        Sounds of Finland -- Qualiton BIS LP 94

YORKSHIRE CAROL
    Wassail Song
        Choir of Leeds Parish Church
        Donald Hunt, cond.
        Christmas At Leeds Parish Church -- Abbey MVP 756

YOUMANS, Vincent (1898-1946)
    Without A Song (from Great Day)
        Lyons Township High School Treble Choir
        Lynne Bradley, dir.
        *Laudate Pueri Dominum a due Cori -- Delta DRS 78M
            720A; Delta DRS 75:423

YOUNG, Gordon (1919-   )
    Now Sing We Joyfully Unto God
        Bethel College Women's Choir
        Oliver Mogck, dir.
        *Gold Cover

    Three Short Psalms (Blessed Is The Man; Hear My Prayer;
            As A Hart Longs for Flowing Streams
        Mississippi University for Women Chapel Choir
        Marilyn Swingle, dir.
        *

ZADOR, Jeno (Eugene) (1894-1977)
    Lonely Wayfarer
        Women's Lyric Club
        Music Library MLR 7095

    Three Rondells
        Women's Lyric Club
        Music Library MLR 7095

ZANINELLI, Luigi (1932-   )
    Americana (from A Folk Song Suite)
        Glen Ellyn Children's Chorus
        Doreen Rao, cond.
        *Delta/Stereo -- DRS 76M 536

    I Know Where I'm Goin'
        Girls Glee of Terry Parker High School
        H. Hampton Kicklighter, dir.
        *Custom Director Records DR 8379-Z4RS 5194

        Lyons Township High School Treble Choir
        Lynne Bradley, dir.
        *(1977) Delta DRS 77M 621

ZINGARELLI, Nicolo (1752-1837)
    Go Not Far From Me, O God
        Bethel College Women's Choir
        Oliver Mogck, dir.
        *Gold Cover

        Lyons Township High School Treble Choir
        Lynne Bradley, dir.
        *Patterns in Music -- Delta DRS 74-139A3

LIST OF PRIVATE RECORDINGS

Advent Records, 23366 Commerce Park Road, Cleveland, Ohio, 44122

The Aeolian Singers, c/o Claire Wall, 6 Lakeview Avenue, Dartmouth, N.S. Canada B3A 3S7

Agnes Scott College Spring Concert 1964, Music Department, Agnes Scott College, Decatur, GA 30030

Alabama Music Educators Association, U.S.C. Sound Enterprise, P.O. Box 11211, Memphis, TN 38111 (copy in library of University of North Carolina - Greensboro)

Bethel College Women's Choir, 3900 Bethel Drive, St. Paul, Minnesota 55112

Cathedral Archive Recordings, c/o Gift Shop, National Cathedral, Washington, D.C.

Choir of Mary Baldwin College, Staunton, Virginia (copy in Howe Library, Shenandoah College & Conservatory of Music)

Choir of St. Thomas Church, 1 West 53rd Street, New York, New York, 10019

Cincinnati BoyChoir, c/o William E. Dickinson, 1310 Sycamore St., Cincinnati, Ohio 45210

Clovis High School Women's Chorus, Clovis High School, Clovis, New Mexico, 88101

Coimbra Records, Highbury Studios, Swan Yard, London N1 15D

Columbus Boychoir Recordings (Talbot Library of Westminster Choir College, Princeton, NJ 08540)

Crest Recordings, 202 Broadway, Huntington Station, New York, 11746

Delta Recordings Mid-West, c/o Lou Everett, 229 11th Avenue, Monroe, Wisconsin 53566

Dorians, c/o Michael Ingham, University of Southern California - Santa Barbara, Santa Barbara, California

145

HIS Recordings, 6811 Norwood Court, New Orleans, Louisiana, 70126

Lyons Township High School Treble Choir, c/o Lynne Bradley, 100 S. Brainard, LaGrange, Illinois 60523

Mennonite Hour Recordings, Media Ministries, 1251 Edom Road, Harrisonburg, VA 22801

Mississippi University for Women Chapel Choir, c/o Marilyn Swingle Music W-250, MUW, Columbus, Mississippi 39701

Moody Bible Institute, 820 LaSalle Drive, Chicago, Illinois, 60610-3285

New Mexico Music Educators Association, Century Stereo, 615 West Adams, Lovington, New Mexico (copy in library of University of North Carolina, Greensboro)

Philomela, c/o Susan Ames-Zierman, Suite 203, 1234 Massachusetts Avenue, N.W., Washington, D.C. 20902 // or // 12001 Judson Road, Wheaton, MD 20902

St. Joseph's Academy, Sister Joan M. Whittemore, Holy Cross Convent, 406 W. White Street, Champaign, Illinois

Salem Academy Glee Club, c/o Jean Burroughs, Salem Academy, Winston-Salem, North Carolina

Salem College Choral Ensembles, Library of Salem College, Winston-Salem, North Carolina

School Sisters of St. Francis, Sister Marie Gnader, 1501 S. Layton Boulevard, Milwaukee, Wisconsin, 53215

Shenandoah Chorus Festival of Music, 1966, Virginia Music Camp, Custom Stereo of Saugus, California (copy in Howe Library, Shenandoah College & Conservatory of Music)

Singing Sargents, Bolling Air Force Base, Washington, D.C. 20332

Songs of Survival, Peninsula Women's Chorus, c/o Patricia Hennings, 2360 Emerson Street, Palo Alto, CA 94301

Sullins College Choir - (recording located in Talbot Library, Westminster Choir College, Princeton, N.J.)

University Choir, University of North Carolina - Greensboro, Greensboro, North Carolina (various recordings, all found in library of UNC-G)

University Treble Choir, Illinois State University, Normal,
    Illinois, 61761

University of Virginia Women's Chorus, University of Virginia,
    Charlottesville, VA 22903

Washington High School Choirs, 340 First St. S.E., Massilon,
    Ohio 44640

Wells College Choir, c/o Wells College Music Department, Aurora,
    New York, 13026

Westover Glee Club, Westover School, Middlebury, Conn., 06762

Wheaton College Women's Chorale, Wheaton College, Wheaton,
    Illinois 60187

Wheelock College Glee Club, c/o Wheelock Alumnae, 200 Riverway,
    Boston, Mass 02215

WWE/Urana Records, 20 West 22nd St., Room 612, New York, New
    York 10010

BIBLIOGRAPHY

Oja, Carol J., ed. AMERICAN MUSIC RECORDINGS: a discography of
    20th century U.S. Composers, Koussevitzky Music Foundation
    (1982)